HOW TO MAKE *anything* IN A SLOW COOKER

HOW TO MAKE *anything* IN A SLOW COOKER

HAYLEY DEAN

EBURY
PRESS

CONTENTS

6 INTRODUCTION

16 **COMFORT FOOD**

44 **SIMPLE & SATISFYING**

72 **FAKEAWAYS**

106 **FAMILY FAVOURITES**

142 **WEEKEND SPECIALS**

170 **SUNDAY LUNCH**

190 **DESSERTS & DRINKS**

212 INDEX

220 ACKNOWLEDGEMENTS

222 ABOUT THE AUTHOR

INTRODUCTION

WELCOME TO HAYLEY'S WORLD

HELLO, I'M HAYLEY...

You may already know me from my posts on Instagram and TikTok, or from my two air fryer cookbooks. The feedback I received from those books was truly amazing and it inspired me to share more easy recipes. This time, I'm taking you back to where it all began for me... slow cooker recipes.

For those of you who don't already know, here's a little bit about me. I'm a busy (single) mum of two daughters who loves cooking and sharing my recipes online, which I've now been doing for a decade. I've been fortunate enough to turn my passion for cooking from a hobby into a full-time career. I absolutely love what I do. I enjoy experimenting with new recipes and, being a self-taught cook, I've learnt so much over the years.

The slow cooker was the first cooking appliance I ever learnt to cook with. I fell in love with the ease of it – knowing that I could prepare everything in the morning, pop it in the slow cooker, then come home from a busy day to a meal that was ready to serve. I'm so passionate about sharing recipes that are home-cooked, easy to make and super delicious. For me, the slow cooker is a great appliance to help achieve this.

Slow cookers have been popular for some years now, but I do think there is so much more they can do that people don't already know. My aim is to spread the word on everything that this wonderful appliance can do.

I really hope you enjoy cooking the recipes in this book. Please do share any that you make with me on social media as I do love to see what everyone creates. Thank you and see you soon!

WHY I LOVE MY SLOW COOKER

Slow cookers are so popular, I think, because of how easy they make serving up tasty home-cooked meals. We are all busier than ever, whether it be working long hours or looking after family members, and most of us don't have time to spend hours in the kitchen making complicated meals from scratch. A slow cooker allows us to make those delicious, filling meals with such ease as they only require the minimum amount of prep and then the appliance does all the hard work!

Some meals definitely taste better when made in a slow cooker, like a beef stew. The long, slow cooking time makes the meat really tender. But if you set about cooking a stew when you arrived home from work, well, you wouldn't be eating until midnight! With a slow cooker, you can set it up in 'cook' mode in the morning and (providing you follow my safety tips on page 13) leave it to do its thing while you get on with your day. That's something you could never do with a pan on the hob.

What exactly is a slow cooker?

A slow cooker is a small kitchen appliance that is used to simmer food at a constant low temperature for a number of hours. The most basic type of slow cooker has a heating element underneath the base of the pot, while a Crock Pot-style slow cooker heats from the underneath and also the sides. Both types produce the same results: they cook food low and slow, meaning you can get on with life while they take care of the daily meal. And because it's a countertop appliance, a slow cooker can be easily moved around the kitchen or stowed away, making it ideal for a kitchen of any size.

Slow cooker or multi cooker – what's the difference?

The sole purpose of a slow cooker is to cook your food slowly, while a multi cooker offers more functions, such as sautéing and steaming. Depending on the modes that it offers, a multi cooker can take the place of a rice cooker, pressure cooker and even an air fryer. Once you establish how you're going to use it, a slow cooker or a multi cooker can both be an equally great option.

How do I choose the right slow cooker for me?

As there are so many slow cookers available now, choosing the right one can be a bit of a minefield! The first thing to take into consideration is size. The slow cooker needs to fit comfortably on your countertop, so think about the space you have available. Another key thing to consider is how many people you regularly cook for: a slow cooker with a 1.5–3 litre capacity will feed one or two people, while a 3–5 litre capacity will serve four or five people, then a 6.5 litre capacity will feed six to eight people. The most basic models will have both a 'low' and 'high' setting, but the majority of slow cookers have more options, including a 'fry' or 'sear' mode. You might also find it useful to have a 'keep warm' setting – once the programmed cooking time has

elapsed, the slow cooker will automatically flick over to 'keep warm', so if you're ever late home then dinner won't be ruined! There are a few other points to consider, such as whether the pot is dishwasher safe, but as all slow cookers pretty much do the same job, you don't need to buy the most expensive model.

Does a slow cooker really use less energy?

Yes, it does! According to the Energy Saving Trust, a slow cooker is one of the most energy efficient kitchen appliances. Despite being on for long periods of time, they typically cost less to run than an oven and only use the same amount of energy as a standard light bulb. You may even be able to take advantage of cheaper night-time energy by cooking your meals overnight and then simply warming them to serve later on. This has the added benefit of giving the flavours of a dish even more time to develop before serving.

Is it safe to leave a slow cooker on when I'm not around?

The joy of using a slow cooker is that you only need to spend a short amount of time on the initial food prep, then you can leave it to do the cooking without having to stand over it. Because a heating element is involved, however, there are just a few safety points to note:

• Always set the slow cooker on a heatproof surface, such as a granite or tiled countertop. Avoid placing it on a wooden table or surface.

• Make sure there is a good 20–30cm space all the way around the slow cooker to allow the heat to dissipate, so don't place it directly up against a wall, cupboard or other appliance.

• Fill the pot of the slow cooker between one-half and three-quarters full. You don't want to fill the pot so much that it overflows, but you need to avoid all the liquid evaporating and the pot running dry.

• If you're going to be out while the slow cooker is on, pick a recipe that can be cooked on 'low'. Any dish cooked on 'high' may be ready before you return.

How do I make sure my food is properly cooked?

Even though food is cooked at a low temperature in a slow cooker, the length of the cooking time and the steam created inside the pot kills off any bacteria, making food safe to eat. You can always check the internal temperature of any meat and poultry with a digital probe thermometer to be sure that it's reached a safe temperature. For other foods, like potatoes and pasta, you can just remove the lid and check with a knife or fork.

Can I really use less liquid in a slow cooker than a casserole?

Yes! Because a slow cooker has a tightly sealed lid, liquid doesn't evaporate in the same way as it does in a casserole, so there's no need to use as much. The general rule is to add just enough liquid to cover the ingredients.

How do I get food nice and brown?

If your slow cooker has a 'fry' or 'sear' setting, sautéeing your ingredients first kickstarts the cooking process and adds some colour. Alternatively, you can brown any meat or vegetables in a frying pan and then transfer it to the pot of the slow cooker. However, this is an optional stage in any recipe and is not strictly necessary – the food will still cook without being browned first, but it helps to seal meat and caramelises the exterior.

What's the best way to clean a slow cooker?

The best way to clean the pot of the slow cooker is to remove any excess food before it dries, then you can wash the pot with a sponge and warm soapy water. If the food has dried on and you're struggling to remove it, adding a splash of distilled malt vinegar and baking soda to the pot and setting it on a low heat should help to get rid of it. Some slow cooker pots are dishwasher safe too, which is helpful.

MY ESSENTIAL INGREDIENTS

There are a small number of storecupboard ingredients that are key to some of my favourite slow cooker recipes, which I keep in stock as they help me to whip up delicious, filling meals with the minimum of fuss.

Pasta, noodles and rice

It's worth keeping a selection of pasta, noodles and rice in the cupboard as they all work so well in the slow cooker. From tubes, spirals and ribbons to the tiny rice-shaped orzo, pasta can be added to the pot of the slow cooker near to the end of the cooking time so that it cooks in the sauce. Pasta takes longer to cook in a slow cooker than in a pan on the hob, but it's perfect for a one-pot meal. The same applies to noodles, although they're fairly quick to cook in the slow cooker, so you just need to add them towards the end before you're ready to serve up. Rice is brilliant for soaking up flavourful liquids, just make sure that you rinse the rice first before adding it to the slow cooker pot.

Stock pots

These handy stock pots are super concentrated blocks of stock in the form of a jelly. They're great for adding intense flavour to your dish. You don't always need to dilute them in boiling water before adding to the pot of your slow cooker, sometimes they can be dropped straight in.

Worcestershire sauce

A classic condiment that is useful for adding a savoury note to stews and soups. The bottle has a handy stopper, which means you can add just a dash.

Barbecue sauce

Beyond chicken wings and burgers, barbecue sauce is also a really handy cheat ingredient that I use in my Hunter's Chicken (see page 53), Barbecue Pulled Pork Buns (see page 80) and Sloppy Joes (see page 112). The spices and sugar in the sauce make it an excellent glaze for slow-cooked meat.

Curry pastes

A jar of curry paste is one of my favourite shortcuts to flavour. I give my suggestion for what I like to use in any recipe, but you can switch in any style of curry paste that you prefer. I tend to go for a tikka, balti or jalfrezi paste to keep things family friendly, but if you like food hotter then feel free to pick a madras or vindaloo paste. And don't forget the Chinese curry paste! As long as it's unopened, a jar of curry paste keeps for ages in the kitchen cupboard.

Peanut butter

I've said this before, but this is one ingredient that I'll never be without. As well as being excellent spread on toast, peanut butter is the key to a quick satay sauce and my Beef Curry with Potatoes and Peanuts (see page 79).

Wine and sparkling wine

Occasionally I add a splash of wine to the pot when slow-cooking. It's always optional so you can leave it out or use stock or water instead, but wine can add extra depth to a dish. It's a great idea to freeze any small amounts of wine left undrunk so you don't have to open a bottle to cook with. Freeze the wine in an ice-cube tray so you have it there in portions to use when needed.

Cream

I prefer to use Elmlea in recipes even though it's not 'real' cream, as it's much lower in calories. Of course, you can use regular cream but just remember that this will affect the calorie count I've given for the recipe.

Cheese

Cheddar, Parmesan and mozzarella are all up there in my top three cheeses and are probably the ones that I use most often in my slow-cooker dishes. However, any type of cheese works really well in the slow cooker. There are so many others that I love: blue cheese, goat's cheese, Gruyère...

Coconut milk

A tin of coconut milk has a long shelf life, so it's really handy to keep one in the cupboard. It's creamy and rich, which makes it an essential ingredient for Thai-style curries and soups, such as my Satay Chicken Curry Noodles (see page 91) and Thai Green Chicken Curry (see page 97). I tend to buy the 'light' version as it is lower in fat and calories.

Microwaveable rice and grains

Microwaveable rice and grains are ready to serve in a few minutes. Usually the pouches contain enough for two servings, so there's nothing wasted.

CHAPTER

1

COMFORT FOOD

LAMB HOT POT

SERVES 4

This gorgeous hot pot needs just 15 minutes of your time at the start of the cooking for a little bit of frying and stirring, after which you can walk away and get on with other things. I like to use lamb mince with 10% fat for a really rich filling, but you can lower it to 5% fat and it will still be super tasty.

Cooking time: 4 hours 20 minutes on high; 8 hours 20 minutes on low

Preparation time: 15 minutes

Calories: 371 kcals per serving

500g lamb mince (10% fat)

½ tablespoon olive oil

1 onion, finely chopped

2 celery stalks, finely diced

2 carrots, peeled and diced into rough 2cm cubes

4 garlic cloves, crushed

3 thyme sprigs, leaves picked

2 tablespoons tomato purée

2 tablespoons Worcestershire sauce

2 tablespoons plain flour

300ml hot lamb or vegetable stock

300g Maris Piper potatoes, thinly sliced (no need to peel)

Salt and freshly ground black pepper

Season the lamb mince with salt and pepper.

Optional – If it has one, set the slow cooker to 'fry' mode (or use a frying pan on the hob for this stage). Add the olive oil to the pot of the slow cooker or frying pan, then add the lamb mince, breaking up any clumps with a wooden spoon, and cook for 7–8 minutes or until browned. (You can skip this stage, but searing the lamb mince helps to lock in flavour.) Transfer the lamb mince to a bowl and set aside.

Put the onion, celery and carrots in the pot of the slow cooker and cook for 7–8 minutes, or until softened.

Add the garlic, thyme, tomato purée, Worcestershire sauce and flour to the pot, then cook, while stirring, for 30 seconds.

Add the lamb mince to the pot, then pour in the stock.

Arrange the potato slices over the lamb to make a neat layer, overlapping them slightly. Season the potato layer with salt and pepper. Cover the pot with the lid.

Set the slow cooker to 'cook' mode, then turn it either to high and cook for 4 hours or to low and cook for 8 hours.

COOK'S TIP

Slice the potatoes as thinly as you can using your sharpest knife. The thinner the potato slices are cut, the more melty they'll become as they cook in the lamb juices.

FANCY SHEPHERDS' PIE

**SERVES
6**

This is my grown-up version of shepherds' pie, using juicy chunks of lamb rather than mince. After cooking the lamb in the slow cooker, I like to serve them in individual dishes so everyone gets their own mini pie. If you're feeling extra fancy, pipe the mash on top of the lamb to make it really pretty, but spooning the mash on works well too. Just make sure the mash is nice and smooth, with no lumps.

Cooking time: 4 hours 20 minutes on high; 8 hours 20 minutes on low

Preparation time: 10 minutes

Calories: 506 kcals per serving (with shop-bought mash)

800g shoulder of lamb, diced

1½ tablespoons plain flour

½ tablespoon olive oil

1 onion, chopped

2 celery stalks, chopped

2 carrots, peeled and diced

3 tablespoons tomato purée

2 tablespoons tomato ketchup

2 tablespoons Worcestershire sauce

4 rosemary sprigs, leaves picked

3 thyme sprigs, leaves picked

100ml hot lamb or vegetable stock

50ml red wine (or replace with the same amount of stock or water)

1 x 800g pack mashed potato (shop-bought, or you can use homemade)

Salt and freshly ground black pepper

Season the lamb with salt and pepper, then toss the meat in the flour until each piece is evenly coated.

Optional – If it has one, set the slow cooker to 'fry' mode (or use a frying pan on the hob for this stage). Add the olive oil to the pot of the slow cooker or frying pan, then toss in the lamb and cook for 7–8 minutes or until lightly browned. (You can skip this stage, but searing the lamb does lock in the flavour.) Transfer the lamb to a bowl and set aside.

Put the onion, celery and carrots in the pot of the slow cooker and cook on high for 7–8 minutes, or until softened.

Add the lamb to the pot, season with salt and pepper. Add the tomato purée, tomato ketchup, Worcestershire sauce and herbs. Pour in the stock and red wine (if using). Cover the pot with the lid.

Set the slow cooker to 'cook' mode, then turn it either to high and cook for 4 hours or to low and cook for 7–8 hours.

Once cooked, spoon the lamb mixture into individual heatproof containers and top with the mash – you can either spoon or pipe the mash on. Spritz the mash tops with spray oil and then pop the pies under a hot grill or into the air fryer to brown the mash.

COOK'S TIP

Instead of regular mashed potato, you can use sweet potato mash to top the pie. Or you could scatter a little grated Cheddar over the mashed potato topping and melt it under the grill or in the air fryer.

BEEF STEW WITH DUMPLINGS

SERVES 8

The slow and low cooking of the beef results in beautifully tender meat, all in a rich, deep gravy with chunky veg. The dumpling mix couldn't be simpler to make up – you just add water. I serve this beef stew with a squirt of brown sauce on the side, but you could stir a tablespoon through the stew for a subtle tanginess.

- Cooking time: 5 hours 20 minutes on high; 8 hours 20 minutes on low
- Preparation time: 15 minutes
- Calories: 436 kcals per serving (with dumplings)

1kg lean stewing beef or braising steak

1 tablespoon plain flour

½ tablespoon olive oil

1 onion, diced

6 celery stalks, sliced

1kg carrots, roughly chopped

2 leeks, sliced

700g baby potatoes, halved

3 beef stock cubes

1 tablespoon Worcestershire sauce

1 tablespoon tomato purée

1 teaspoon dried thyme

2 bay leaves

4 tablespoons gravy granules (add more or less depending on how thick you prefer the sauce)

1 x 142g packet of dumpling mix (I use Goldenfry Farmhouse Dumpling Mix)

Salt and freshly ground black pepper

Season the beef with salt and pepper, then toss the meat in the flour until each piece is evenly coated.

Optional – If it has one, set the slow cooker to 'fry' mode (or use a frying pan on the hob for this stage). Add the olive oil to the pot of the slow cooker or frying pan, then toss in the beef and cook for 7–8 minutes or until lightly browned. (You can skip this stage, but searing the beef does lock in the flavour.) Transfer the beef to a bowl and set aside.

Put the onion, celery, carrots, leeks and potatoes in the pot of the slow cooker and cook on high for 7–8 minutes.

Add the beef to the pot, season with salt and pepper, then crumble in the stock cubes. Add the Worcestershire sauce, tomato purée, thyme and bay leaves. Pour in just enough water to cover the ingredients. Cover the pot with the lid.

Set the slow cooker to 'cook' mode, then turn it either to high and cook for 5 hours or to low and cook for 8 hours.

Once cooked, stir in the gravy granules to thicken the sauce to your liking.

Before serving, make up the dumpling mix following the packet instructions and mould into 8 equal-sized dumplings. Put them in the slow cooker pot on top of the stew and cook for the last 30 minutes of the cooking time or until the dumplings have risen, expanded in size and are cooked through.

COOK'S TIP

To crisp up the dumplings, pop them under a hot grill. If the pot of your slow cooker is heatproof, place it directly under the grill. Otherwise, lift the dumplings out and place them in a heatproof dish.

KEEMA CURRY

This tasty curry uses beef mince and just a handful of other ingredients, making it an easy week-night option. The word keema translates as 'minced meat' – traditionally lamb mince is used in India, but it works equally well with beef. I use a jar of curry paste for ease, but you could experiment with ground spices. Most curries taste better the day after they're made, and this one's no exception.

 Cooking time: 4 hours 35 minutes on high; 8 hours 35 minutes on low

 Preparation time: 10 minutes

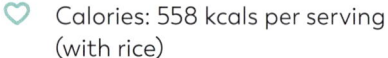 Calories: 558 kcals per serving (with rice)

500g beef mince (5% fat)

1 onion, diced

1 red pepper, diced

2 tablespoons tikka masala paste (I use Patak's)

1 tablespoon tomato purée

1 teaspoon garlic paste

1 teaspoon sugar

1 x 500ml carton passata

200g frozen petit pois (or garden peas)

Salt and freshly ground black pepper

To serve

300g basmati rice

1 small red chilli, finely sliced

Season the beef mince with salt and pepper.

Optional – If it has one, set the slow cooker to 'fry' mode (or use a frying pan on the hob for this stage). Add the beef mince to the pot of the slow cooker or frying pan and cook in the pan for 7–8 minutes or until lightly browned. (You can skip this stage, but searing the beef mince does helps to lock in the flavour.) Transfer the beef mince to a bowl and set aside.

Put the onion and red pepper in the pot of the slow cooker and cook on high for 7–8 minutes, or until softened.

Add the tikka masala paste, tomato purée, garlic paste and sugar to the pot. Cook, while stirring, for 30 seconds.

Return the beef mince to the pot, then pour in the passata. Fill the empty passata carton one-quarter full with water, swirl it around and add that to the pot and give everything a good stir. Cover the pot with the lid.

Set the slow cooker to 'cook' mode, then either turn it to high and cook for 4 hours or turn it to low and cook for 8 hours. (If you need to, the keema curry can be left on low for up to 10 hours.)

Once cooked, stir the frozen petit pois or garden peas into the keema. Put the lid back on the pot and cook for a further 15 minutes.

Before serving, cook the rice following the packet instructions. Scatter the finely chopped red chilli over the keema and serve it spooned on top of the rice.

SAUSAGE AND ONION CASSEROLE WITH MASHED POTATOES

SERVES
4

A bowl full of creamy mash topped with sausages cooked in an onion gravy is my perfect comfort food when the weather is chilly. As an alternative to mash, sometimes I serve this casserole in a giant Yorkshire pudding, which I make in my air fryer.

Cooking time: 4 hours 15 minutes on high; 8 hours 15 minutes on low

Preparation time: 15 minutes

Calories: 572 kcals per serving (with mash)

8 pork sausages (you can use reduced fat, if you prefer)

1 onion, diced

500g carrots, roughly chopped

2 leeks, sliced

1 tablespoon tomato purée

½ teaspoon rosemary leaves

½ teaspoon thyme leaves

1 bay leaf

1 tablespoon Worcestershire sauce

500ml hot beef stock

3 tablespoons gravy granules

Salt and freshly ground black pepper

For the mash

1kg potatoes, peeled and cut into large chunks

Knob of butter

Optional – If it has one, set the slow cooker to 'fry' mode (or use a non-stick frying pan over a low–medium heat for this stage). Add the sausages to the dry pot of the slow cooker or pan and cook for 5 minutes or until lightly browned. (You can skip this stage, but searing the sausages does help to lock in the flavour.) Transfer the sausages to a bowl and set aside.

Put the onion, carrots, leeks, tomato purée and herbs in the pot of the slow cooker and cook on high for 10 minutes, or until softened.

Add the sausages to the pot along with the Worcestershire sauce. Pour in the stock. Cover the pot with the lid.

Set the slow cooker to 'cook' mode, then turn it either to high and cook for 4 hours or to low and cook for 8 hours.

Once cooked, stir in the gravy granules to thicken the sauce. (You can add more or less granules, depending on how thick you like the sauce. Just remember, it will thicken up further when left overnight.)

With 15 minutes of the cooking time left, make the mash. Place the potatoes in a large pan of salted water. Bring to the boil over a high heat and cook the potatoes for about 15 minutes or until they're soft enough to mash. Once cooked, drain the potatoes, return them to the pan and roughly mash them. Add the knob of butter and continue to mash until smooth. Season the mash to your taste.

When ready to serve, spoon some mash into individual bowls and then place the sausage casserole on top, making sure everyone gets two sausages each.

SAUSAGE RAGÙ WITH RIGATONI

SERVES 4

This is a brilliantly versatile yet simple pasta dish. I use regular pork sausages for maximum flavour, but you can swap them for reduced fat ones, if you like. And if you want to switch up the flavour of the ragù at any time, try adding a teaspoon of fennel seeds with the garlic – sausage and fennel is a classic Italian pairing. Or a really simple way to ring the changes is to use a flavoured sausage – Italian-style herb or chorizo-style sausages are both good options.

Cooking time: 3 hours 20 minutes on high; 7 hours 20 minutes on low

Preparation time: 10 minutes

Calories: 600 kcals per serving

6 pork sausages (you can use reduced fat, if you prefer)

1 onion, diced

4 garlic cloves, crushed

1 teaspoon dried oregano

2 tablespoons tomato purée

100ml red wine

1 x 400g tin chopped tomatoes

70ml milk

1 teaspoon sugar

200g rigatoni (or any other tube-shaped pasta)

1 tablespoon double cream (I use Elmlea)

15g Parmesan, grated, plus extra to serve

Optional – If it has one, set the slow cooker to 'fry' mode (or use a non-stick frying pan over a low–medium heat for this stage). Add the sausage meat to the pot of the slow cooker or frying pan with a splash of olive oil, squeezing the meat out of the skins to break it up. Leave it to sit in the pot for a minute, without stirring, so the meat starts to brown, then cook for 5–6 minutes. (You can skip this stage, but searing the sausage meat helps to lock in the flavour.)

Put the onion in the pot of the slow cooker with the sausage meat and cook on high for 7–8 minutes, or until softened.

Add the garlic, oregano and tomato purée to the pot, then cook, while stirring, for 1 minute.

Pour in the red wine and cook until nearly all the liquid has evaporated (about 1 minute), then add the chopped tomatoes, milk and sugar. Cover the pot with the lid.

Set the slow cooker to 'cook' mode, then turn it either to high and cook for 2 hours or to low and cook for 4 hours.

Next, add the pasta to the pot along with 100ml boiling water, then stir to combine. Cover the pot with the lid and cook for a further 1 hour.

When ready to serve, stir through the double cream and grated Parmesan. Spoon the sausage ragù and pasta into individual bowls and scatter over a little extra Parmesan.

PORK STEW WITH APPLES AND CIDER

SERVES 4

This hearty pork dish is creamy and comforting. It's great served with a slightly looser sauce – like a stew – along with a soft bread roll for mopping up the sauce, or you can reduce the liquid further to make it a bit thicker and then spoon it over mash. Both ways are gorgeous, so I'll leave it up to you to decide.

 Cooking time: 3 hours 15 minutes on high; 6 hours 15 minutes on low

 Preparation time: 5 minutes

 Calories: 596 kcals per serving (without mash or bread)

80g bacon lardons

600g pork shoulder, cut into rough 2cm cubes

2 tablespoons plain flour

1 onion, finely chopped

2 celery stalks, finely chopped

1 carrot, peeled and diced

2 eating apples, cored and sliced

320ml cider

1 chicken stock pot

1–2 teaspoons cornflour

2 tablespoons half-fat crème fraîche

1 tablespoon Dijon mustard

Salt and freshly ground black pepper

Optional – If it has one, set the slow cooker to 'fry' mode (or use a frying pan over a low–medium heat for this stage). Chuck the bacon lardons into the pot of the slow cooker or frying pan and cook for 2–3 minutes or until browned. Transfer the lardons to a plate and set aside.

Season the pork with salt and pepper, then toss in the flour until each piece is evenly coated. Add the pork to the pot and cook on high for 2–3 minutes or until browned.

Add the lardons to the pot along with any remaining flour, then add the onion, celery, carrot, apples, cider and stock pot. Cover the pot with the lid.

Set the slow cooker to 'cook' mode, then turn it either to high and cook for 3 hours or to low and cook for 6 hours.

Remove a tablespoon of the sauce and combine with the cornflour in a small bowl. Stir half of this cornflour mixture back into the sauce in the pot. Continue to cook, with the lid off, for a further 5 minutes. If you want to thicken the sauce a little more, stir in the remaining cornflour mixture.

When ready to serve, stir the crème fraîche and mustard into the sauce.

COOK'S TIP

If you prefer the dish to have a little extra punch, add some more mustard to suit your taste.

CREAMY PAPRIKA CHICKEN WITH MUSHROOMS

If you enjoy the flavours of a beef stroganoff, then you'll love my creamy paprika chicken with mushrooms as it has all the same key flavours. Using chicken makes it a lighter meal, ideal for weekday evenings, plus chicken is more affordable compared to steak. I sometimes serve this recipe with rice, then at other times with garlic bread, but you could always double up on the carbs and have both.

Cooking time: 2 hours on high; 4 hours on low

Preparation time: 10 minutes, plus marinating

Calories: 205 kcals per serving (without rice or garlic bread)

3 skinless chicken breasts (about 450g), diced

1 teaspoon garlic paste

2 teaspoons paprika, plus an extra pinch to serve

1 onion, diced

250g mushrooms, sliced (I use chestnut mushrooms)

1 chicken stock pot or cube mixed with 125ml boiling water

3 tablespoons half-fat crème fraîche

30g Parmesan, grated

½ teaspoon dried parsley

Salt and freshly ground black pepper

Put the chicken in a bowl with the garlic paste, paprika and plenty of salt and pepper. Mix well, making sure all the chicken pieces are evenly coated. Cover the bowl with clingfilm and leave to marinate in the fridge for at least 10 minutes, but preferably longer – up to 1 hour, if you have the time.

Put the marinated chicken in the pot of the slow cooker along with the onion and mushrooms. Pour in the stock, then stir well to combine. Cover the pot with the lid.

Set the slow cooker to 'cook' mode, then either turn it to high and cook for 2 hours or turn it to low and cook for 4 hours.

With 30 minutes of the cooking time left, stir in the crème fraîche, grated Parmesan and dried parsley.

When ready to serve, sprinkle over an extra pinch of paprika.

COOK'S TIP

I use regular paprika, but you could swap in smoked sweet or smoked hot paprika, depending on what you like best.

SMOKY FISH PIE

SERVES 6

This is a kind of upside-down fish pie, with the mashed potato on the bottom and the rich, creamy, smoky fish filling on top. I use a combination of smoked salmon, smoked haddock, cod and prawns – if you prefer to leave any of these out, please do. You could also use a frozen fish pie mixture as well as microwaveable mash if you want to save time.

Cooking time: 3 hours 15 minutes on low

Preparation time: 5 minutes

Calories: 486 kcals per serving (with mash)

50g unsalted butter

50g plain flour

450ml whole milk

150g cream cheese (I use Philadelphia)

50g Cheddar, grated

100g smoked salmon, cut into strips

240g smoked haddock, skin removed and cut into rough 2cm chunks

320g cod, cut into rough 2cm chunks

165g king prawns

200g frozen garden peas, defrosted in hot water

10g fresh parsley, chopped

1 x 800g pack mashed potato (shop-bought, or you can use homemade)

Salt and freshly ground black pepper

Set the slow cooker to high (or use a saucepan over a medium heat for this stage). Melt the butter in the pot of the slow cooker or pan, then beat in the flour using a wooden spoon. Slowly add the milk, beating as you go, to make a smooth sauce. Stir in the cream cheese and grated Cheddar to make a cheese sauce.

Put the salmon, haddock and cod in the pot and season well with salt and pepper. Cover the pot with the lid.

Set the slow cooker to 'cook' mode, then turn it to low and cook for 3 hours.

With 5 minutes of the cooking time left, add the prawns, peas and most of the chopped parsley.

When ready to serve, heat the mash following the packet instructions. Serve the fish pie filling on top of the mash and sprinkled with the remaining parsley. Alternatively, transfer the fish pie mixture to a heatproof dish, top with the warm mash, then finish it off under a hot grill for some crunch and colour.

COOK'S TIP

You can easily turn this fish pie into a gratin. Instead of topping with mash, scatter breadcrumbs over the fish mixture along with some grated cheese – Parmesan, Gruyère and Cheddar are all great choices – and then place it under a hot grill for 8–10 minutes.

VEGGIE MOUSSAKA

A light yet comforting meal, this veggie moussaka makes a delicious summer lunch, eaten outdoors. Packed with loads of seasonal veg – courgettes, peppers and aubergines – it also includes layers of thinly sliced potato to make it a filling, all-in-one meal. You don't need to serve it with anything else, but if you want to, a crisp side salad goes nicely alongside.

Cooking time: 3 hours 15 minutes on high; 5 hours 45 minutes on low

Preparation time: 10 minutes

Calories: 272 kcals per serving

2 tablespoons olive oil

2 aubergines, sliced into 1cm thick discs

2 peppers (any colour – I use red), cut into bite-sized chunks

1 large courgette, diced

1 red onion, chopped

2 garlic cloves, crushed

2 tablespoons tomato purée

1 teaspoon dried mixed herbs

1 teaspoon ground cinnamon

1 teaspoon sugar

1 x 500ml carton passata

2 medium potatoes, peeled and thinly sliced

Salt and freshly ground black pepper

For the topping

250ml natural yoghurt

2 eggs, beaten

Pinch of ground nutmeg (optional)

50g Parmesan, grated

To serve

Side salad

If it has one, set the slow cooker to 'fry' mode (or use a frying pan on the hob for this stage). Add 1 tablespoon of the olive oil to the pot of the slow cooker or frying pan and then, working in batches, add the aubergine slices and cook for 2 minutes on each side, or until golden. Add a little more oil to the pan for the next batch, if needed. Transfer the aubergine slices to a plate and set aside.

Put the peppers, courgette and onion in the pot of the slow cooker with the remaining oil and cook on high for 4 minutes, or until slightly softened.

Add the garlic, tomato purée, mixed herbs, cinnamon and sugar to the pot. Pour in the passata, then stir well to mix everything together.

Scoop half of the vegetable mixture out of the pot and set aside in a bowl. Arrange half of the aubergine slices in a layer on top of the vegetable mixture left in the pot, followed by a layer of half of the potato slices.

Return the remaining vegetable mixture to the pot, spooning it on top of the potato layer. Finish with the remaining aubergine slices and potato slices. Cover the pot with the lid.

Set the slow cooker to 'cook' mode, then turn it either to high and cook for 2 hours 30 minutes or to low and cook for 5 hours.

To make the topping, combine the yoghurt, eggs and nutmeg (if using) in a small bowl, then season to taste with salt and pepper. Spoon this yoghurt mixture on top of the moussaka, then scatter over the grated Parmesan and cook on high for 30 minutes.

When ready, spoon the moussaka into bowls and serve with a crisp side salad.

MUSHROOM AND MIXED BEAN STEW

If you're trying to cut down the amount of meat you eat, but you still want something hearty and comforting, this is the recipe to turn to. Mushrooms provide so much flavour as well as containing lots of protein. Using tins of mixed beans is a great shortcut as there is no soaking or rinsing required, just make sure that you get the ones in water and not vinaigrette.

Cooking time: 2 hours 45 minutes on high; 4 hours 45 minutes on low

Preparation time: 10 minutes

Calories: 409 kcals per serving (without mash or veg)

2 tablespoons olive oil

1 onion, finely chopped

2 celery stalks, finely chopped

250g chestnut mushrooms, sliced

250g button mushrooms, halved

1 tablespoon flour

2 x 400g tins mixed beans in water, drained

300ml hot chicken stock

6 thyme sprigs, leaves picked

1 tablespoon cornflour

150ml double cream (I use Elmlea)

1½ tablespoons Dijon mustard

2 teaspoons white wine vinegar

To serve

10g parsley or chives, finely chopped

Mashed potatoes (shop-bought or homemade)

Your choice of green vegetables

If it has one, set the slow cooker to 'fry' mode (or use a non-stick frying pan over a medium heat for this stage). Add the olive oil to the pot of the slow cooker or frying pan, chuck in the onion and celery and cook for 5 minutes or until slightly softened.

Put the mushrooms in the pot of the slow cooker or frying pan and cook on high for 5–7 minutes, or until lightly browned, then sprinkle in the flour and cook for a further 1 minute.

Tip the mixed beans into the pot of the slow cooker. Pour in the hot stock and scatter in the thyme leaves. Cover the pot with the lid.

Set the slow cooker to 'cook' mode, then turn it either to high and cook for 2 hours or to low and cook for 4 hours.

Remove 2 tablespoons of the sauce and combine with the cornflour in a small bowl. Stir half of this cornflour mixture back into the sauce in the pot. Continue to cook, with the lid off, for a further 5 minutes. If you want to thicken the sauce a little more, stir in the rest of the cornflour mixture.

Next, stir the cream, mustard and vinegar into the stew, then continue to cook on high, uncovered, for 30 minutes.

When ready to serve, stir the chopped parsley or chives through the stew and season to taste. Serve the stew with the mash and your choice of veggies.

BUTTERNUT SQUASH AND SPINACH DAAL

SERVES 6

This veggie daal is a cosy hug in a bowl – super comforting on those days when you fancy a meat-free meal. You can adjust the spices used here based on whatever you have in your cupboard or spice rack. Even just using a teaspoonful of curry powder makes a really tasty daal.

Cooking time: 4 hours 10 minutes on high; 8 hours 10 minutes on low

Preparation time: 10 minutes

Calories: 359 kcals per serving

2 onions, chopped

½ tablespoon sunflower oil or coconut oil

6 garlic cloves, crushed

Thumb-sized piece of ginger, peeled and finely chopped

1 tablespoon garam masala

2 teaspoons medium curry powder

1 teaspoon chilli flakes

Half a large butternut squash (about 500g), peeled and diced into 1.5cm cubes

400g green lentils, rinsed

400g red lentils, soaked in boiling water for 10 minutes then rinsed

1 x 400g tin chopped tomatoes

1 x 400ml tin light coconut milk

150g frozen spinach

Salt and freshly ground black pepper

To serve

2 tablespoons natural yoghurt

Pinch of chilli flakes

10g coriander leaves, torn (optional)

Optional – If it has one, set the slow cooker to 'fry' mode (or use a frying pan on the hob for this stage). Put the onions and oil in the pan and cook for 7–8 minutes, or until softened. (You can skip this stage, but frying the onions does helps to kickstart the caramelisation process.)

Put the garlic, ginger, spices and chilli flakes in the pot of the slow cooker along with the onions and fry for 1 minute, or until fragrant.

Add the butternut squash, green and red lentils and chopped tomatoes to the pot. Pour in the coconut milk along with 400ml water, then season well with salt and pepper. Cover the pot with the lid.

Set the slow cooker to 'cook' mode, then turn it either to high and cook for 4 hours or to low and cook for 8 hours.

When ready to serve, stir the frozen spinach through the daal until it has wilted and been incorporated.

Spoon the daal into bowls and top each with a dollop of yoghurt and a scattering of chilli flakes and coriander leaves (if using).

COOK'S TIP

This is a really useful recipe for using up whatever spices you have to hand. Instead of curry powder, you could add ground turmeric, cumin seeds, mustard seeds and dried curry leaves for a really aromatic daal.

SWEET POTATO AND RED LENTIL STEW

SERVES
4

This comforting stew is sweet and smoky, but not too spicy. Soaking the red lentils before you add them to the slow cooker is important as it kickstarts the cooking process and ensures they lose their bite. The sweet potato cooks to a lovely light texture in the slow cooker – just don't cut the chunks too small as you don't want them to disappear. This is a handy all-in-one dish, so you don't need anything on the side.

Cooking time: 4 hours 10 minutes on high; 9 hours 10 minutes on low

Preparation time: 10 minutes, plus soaking

Calories: 361 kcals per serving

½ tablespoon olive oil

3 red peppers, sliced

1 red onion, thinly sliced

3 garlic cloves, crushed

3 tablespoons tomato purée

2 teaspoons chipotle chilli flakes

1½ teaspoons sweet smoked paprika

1 tablespoon white wine vinegar

1 teaspoon sugar

1 large sweet potato (about 350g), peeled and cut into rough 2cm chunks

250g red lentils, soaked in boiling water for 10 minutes then rinsed

1 x 400g tin chopped tomatoes

400ml hot vegetable stock

Soured cream, to serve (optional)

Optional – If it has one, set the slow cooker to 'fry' mode (or use a frying pan over a medium heat for this stage). Add the olive oil to the pot of the slow cooker or frying pan, then throw in the red peppers and onion and cook for 7–8 minutes, or until softened.

Add the garlic, tomato purée, chipotle chilli flakes and paprika to the pot along with the peppers and onion, then cook for 3 minutes or until fragrant.

Stir in the vinegar and sugar, then add the sweet potato, lentils and chopped tomatoes. Pour in the stock. Cover the pot with the lid.

Set the slow cooker to 'cook' mode, then either turn it to high and cook for 4 hours or turn it to low and cook for 9 hours, or until the lentils no longer have much bite.

When ready to serve, ladle the stew into bowls and top with a dollop of soured cream (if using).

COOK'S TIP

If you don't have 10 minutes to soak the lentils, you could cook them for longer in the slow cooker, but the sweet potato chunks may break down into the lentils.

MEXICAN-STYLE VEGGIE CHILLI

SERVES 4-6

Warming, smoky and spicy, this veggie chilli contains two types of beans which means it's packed with protein. Using a tin of kidney beans in chilli sauce is a handy shortcut to extra flavour. And on that topic, you could chuck in the whole sachet of fajita seasoning and leave out the smoked paprika, if you don't have any paprika in the cupboard. This chilli is great served on rice, then any leftovers can be used for nachos.

⏲ Cooking time: 4 hours 10 minutes on high; 8 hours 10 minutes on low

🥄 Preparation time: 10 minutes

♡ Calories: 506 kcals per serving (based on 4 servings, with rice, avocado and soured cream)

½ tablespoon olive oil

2 red peppers, cut into strips

1 small onion, chopped

3 garlic cloves, crushed

½ x 30g sachet fajita seasoning

2 teaspoons smoked paprika

1 x 400g tin kidney beans in chilli sauce

1 x 400g tin black beans, drained

1 x 400g tin chopped tomatoes

2 tablespoons tomato purée

2 teaspoons mixed herbs

100ml hot vegetable stock

To serve

2 x 250g pouches microwave basmati rice

2 tablespoons soured cream

1 avocado, sliced

Small handful of coriander (optional)

Optional – If it has one, set the slow cooker to 'fry' mode (or use a frying pan on the hob for this stage). Add the olive oil to the pot of the slow cooker or frying pan, then toss in the red peppers and onion and cook for 7–8 minutes, or until softened. (You can skip this stage, but frying the onions does help to kickstart the caramelisation process.)

Put the garlic, fajita seasoning and smoked paprika in the pot along with the red peppers and onions, followed by the kidney beans (including the sauce), black beans, chopped tomatoes, tomato purée and mixed herbs. Pour over the stock, then stir to mix everything together. Cover the pan with the lid.

Set the slow cooker to 'cook' mode, then turn it either to high and cook for 4 hours or to low and cook for 7–8 hours. If you're around, stir the contents of the pan once during the cooking time.

When ready to serve, prepare the rice following the packet instructions. Divide the rice between serving bowls, then spoon the chilli on top. Add a dollop of soured cream and a few avocado slices to each bowl, then scatter over a few coriander leaves (if using).

COOK'S TIP

This may sound unusual, but trust me on this. A couple of squares of dark chocolate stirred through the chilli just before serving gives the dish a lovely richness and slightly bitter note. Or you could just eat the chocolate instead!

CHAPTER
2

SIMPLE & SATISFYING

FRENCH ONION AND STEAK SOUP

SERVES 4

Slivers of tender steak make this onion soup really flavourful. And the Gruyère toast that sits on the surface takes the soup to another level. It's just sooo good. It's a really filling meal so you can happily serve a bowlful as a main dish, or you could serve a small amount as a starter to dinner guests. If you want to impress, the brandy gives the soup a lovely warmth, but you can easily leave it out.

 Cooking time: 4 hours 30 minutes on high; 8 hours 30 minutes on low

 Preparation time: 10 minutes

♡ Calories: 343 kcals per serving (with Gruyère toast)

2 sirloin steaks (about 450g), trimmed of any fat and sliced into thin strips widthways

1 tablespoon flour, seasoned

1½ tablespoons olive oil

3 large onions (about 700g), thinly sliced

3 garlic cloves, crushed

1 teaspoon sugar

1 tablespoon brandy (optional)

2 teaspoons wholegrain mustard, plus extra to spread on toast

4 thyme sprigs, leaves picked

800ml hot beef stock

4 slices of bread, toasted

90g Gruyère, grated

Salt and freshly ground black pepper

Season the steak with salt and pepper, then toss the meat in the flour until each piece is evenly coated.

Optional – If it has one, set the slow cooker to 'fry' mode (or use a frying pan over a medium heat for this stage). Add ½ tablespoon of the olive oil to the pot of the slow cooker or frying pan, then tumble in the steak and cook for 3–4 minutes, or until lightly browned. Transfer the steak to a bowl with any remaining flour and set aside.

Add the remaining 1 tablespoon of olive oil to the pot of the slow cooker, then add the onions, season with salt and cook on high for 10–12 minutes, or until softened.

Add the garlic, sugar and brandy (if using), then cook for a further 1 minute. Stir in the mustard and thyme, then pour in the beef stock. Add the steak to the pot, then season well with salt and pepper. Cover the pot with the lid.

Set the slow cooker to 'cook' mode, then turn it either to high and cook for 4 hours or to low and cook for 8 hours.

Turn the slow cooker to high. Spread the slices of toast with a little wholegrain mustard, float them on top of the soup, mustard side up, and sprinkle with the grated Gruyère. Put the lid back on and cook for a further 15 minutes.

COOK'S TIP

If you can, use slightly stale bread for the Gruyère toast as the bread goes soft in the soup anyway. Stale sourdough works especially well.

PEA AND HAM SOUP

When it comes to soup, this is an absolute classic flavour combination. If you grow your own, you could use fresh peas for the pure taste of summer, but you can enjoy this soup all year round by grabbing a bag of frozen peas. The broth is nicely seasoned by the gammon so you shouldn't need to add any extra salt.

⏲ Cooking time: 4 hours 10 minutes on high; 8 hours 10 minutes on low

🍳 Preparation time: 5 minutes

♡ Calories: 272 kcals per serving (based on 4 servings)

1 potato (about 175g), peeled and diced

1 onion, chopped

2 leeks, thinly sliced

450g unsmoked gammon joint

1 litre hot vegetable stock

400g frozen garden peas, defrosted in hot water

2 tablespoons natural yoghurt (optional)

Put the potato, onion, leeks and gammon in the pot of the slow cooker. Pour over the stock. Cover the pot with the lid.

Set the slow cooker to 'cook' mode, then turn it either to high and cook for 4 hours or to low and cook for 8 hours.

Add the peas to the pot and cook for a further 10 minutes.

Once cooked, transfer the gammon to a plate and shred it into thin strips.

Using a handheld stick blender, blitz the soup until smooth.

Ladle the soup into bowls, drizzle over the yoghurt (if using) and top with the shredded ham.

PEPPERONI PIZZA ORZO

This pasta dish is so simple, but mega delicious! Pepperoni is one of my go-to pizza choices, but the recipe can be easily adapted to include your favourite pizza topping. For example, you could scrap the pepperoni slices in favour of more peppers or some leftover roasted veggies to make it meat-free.

Cooking time: 1 hour 5 minutes on high

Preparation time: 5 minutes

Calories: 476 kcals per serving

250g orzo

1 red onion, chopped

2 small peppers (any colour), diced

2 teaspoons dried mixed herbs

350ml tomato and basil pizza sauce

350ml boiling water

140g mozzarella and Cheddar mixture, grated

50g pepperoni, thinly sliced

Handful of basil leaves, torn, to serve

Put the orzo, onion, peppers and mixed herbs in the pot of the slow cooker. Pour over the pizza sauce and boiling water. Cover the pot with the lid.

Set the slow cooker to 'cook' mode, turn it to high and cook for 1 hour.

Stir the orzo in the pot, adding a splash of water if needed, then fold through half of the grated cheese. Scatter the remaining cheese over the top and arrange the pepperoni slices evenly over the surface. Cook the orzo for a further 5 minutes.

When ready to serve, scatter with some torn basil leaves.

HUNTER'S CHICKEN

SERVES 4

I love finding new ways of making Hunter's Chicken, so this is my slow-cooker version. Wrapping the chicken breasts in bacon keeps the meat super succulent so that it stays really moist during the long, slow cook. This dish has so much flavour that people really won't believe it's made from just five ingredients.

- Cooking time: 3 hours 15 minutes on high; 6 hours 15 minutes on low
- Preparation time: 10 minutes
- Calories: 482 kcals per serving (without chips or mash)

4 skinless chicken breasts (about 600g)

8 streaky bacon rashers

150ml barbecue sauce

1 tablespoon cornflour

100g mozzarella and Cheddar mixture, grated

Wrap each chicken breast in 2 bacon rashers and put them in the pot of the slow cooker. Spread each chicken breast with a generous amount of the barbecue sauce. Cover the pot with the lid.

Set the slow cooker to 'cook' mode, then turn it either to high and cook for 3 hours or to low and cook for 6 hours.

Remove 1 tablespoon of the barbecue sauce mixture and combine with the cornflour in a small bowl. Stir this cornflour mixture back into the sauce in the pot (carefully remove the chicken breasts to do this, if needed).

Top the chicken breasts with the grated cheese, place the lid back on the pot, then continue to cook on high for a further 15 minutes.

When ready, serve the hunter's chicken with either oven chips or sweet potato mash, if you like.

CHICKEN NOODLE SOUP

SERVES 4

This beautifully light soup is so fragrant – it makes the kitchen smell amazing while it's slow cooking. Although it's really easy to put together, you could always cook the broth a day ahead so that it's ready to serve the next day. Or you can make a large batch of broth and then freeze it in portions.

Cooking time: 2 hours 30 minutes on high; 5 hours on low

Preparation time: 5 minutes

Calories: 274 kcals per serving

For the soup

3 spring onions, sliced (save the green parts to serve)

Thumb sized piece of ginger, peeled and sliced

4 garlic cloves, sliced

2 star anise

1 red chilli, sliced

2 skinless chicken breasts (about 300g)

2 carrots, peeled and cut into 1cm dice

1 banana shallot, chopped

800ml hot chicken stock

3 tablespoons sweet chilli sauce

To finish

125g rice vermicelli noodles

1 x 198g tin sweetcorn kernels, drained

15g coriander and mint leaves, finely chopped

2 tablespoons crispy onions

1 lime, cut into wedges, to serve (optional)

Chilli oil, to serve (optional)

Add all the ingredients for the soup (except the green parts of the spring onions) to the pot of the slow cooker. Cover the pot with the lid.

Set the slow cooker to 'cook' mode, then turn it either to high and cook for 2 hours 30 minutes or to low and cook for 5 hours.

When ready to serve, put the noodles in a heatproof bowl and cover with boiling water. Let sit for 4 minutes (or follow the packet instructions), then drain.

Meanwhile, lift the chicken breasts out of the slow cooker and shred the meat.

Divide the noodles between four serving bowls. Do the same with the sweetcorn kernels and shredded chicken, then spoon the hot broth over the top.

Garnish the soup with the spring onion greens, chopped herbs and crispy onions. Serve with lime wedges to squeeze over and some chilli oil, if you like.

COOK'S TIP

If you prefer, you could always spoon the broth over some steamed or microwaved rice instead of noodles.

CAJUN-STYLE CHICKEN SPAGHETTI

SERVES 4

The smoky spice of Cajun seasoning is a heavenly match for chicken. And if you know how much I love pasta, well, it was a no-brainer for me to put all these ingredients together to create this easy, delicious dinner! This is amazing served with a dressed salad and some garlic bread, of course.

Cooking time: 1 hour 30 minutes on high

Preparation time: 10 minutes

Calories: 499 kcals per serving

500g skinless chicken breasts, diced

1 onion, diced

1 pepper (any colour – I use ½ green and ½ red), sliced

1 teaspoon garlic paste

3 teaspoons Cajun seasoning

Pinch of chilli flakes

1 x 500ml carton passata

90g cream cheese

300g spaghetti

1 teaspoon chopped parsley

Salt and freshly ground black pepper

Put the chicken, onion, pepper and garlic paste in the pot of the slow cooker. Sprinkle over the Cajun seasoning, chilli flakes and a pinch each of salt and pepper.

Pour the passata into the pot, then stir well to mix everything together. Cover the pot with the lid.

Set the slow cooker to 'cook' mode, then turn it to high and cook for 40–50 minutes, or until the chicken is cooked through.

Add the cream cheese to the pot, then stir through the chicken mixture.

Add the spaghetti along with a splash of water, and stir well again. Cook for a further 40 minutes or until the pasta is cooked, topping up with a splash more water, if needed.

When ready to serve, divide the pasta between bowls and scatter over the parsley.

CHUNKY BAKED BEANS

If you're thinking, 'Why on earth would I make baked beans when I can open a tin', think again. These Chunky Baked Beans are nothing like the beans you might serve with a Full English (although I love those too). They're more a rustic dish of butter beans with smoky bacon, paprika and rosemary. Serve these beans on a slice of buttered toast or a baked potato, topped with grated Parmesan.

Cooking time: 3 hours 5 minutes on high; 5 hours 5 minutes on low

Preparation time: 10 minutes

Calories: 340 kcals per serving (without toast or jacket potato)

½ tablespoon vegetable oil

150g smoked bacon lardons

1 teaspoon sweet smoked paprika

1 carrot, finely chopped

2 celery stalks, finely chopped

2 garlic cloves, crushed

2 tablespoons tomato purée

½ tablespoon red wine vinegar

½ tablespoon sugar

1 x 400g tin chopped tomatoes

2 x 400g tins butter beans, drained

2 rosemary sprigs, finely chopped

Parmesan cheese, grated (optional)

Salt and freshly ground black pepper

Optional – If it has one, set the slow cooker to 'fry' mode (or use a frying pan over a medium heat for this stage). Add the vegetable oil to the pot of the slow cooker or frying pan, then toss in the bacon lardons and cook for 4 minutes or until golden brown. Next, add the paprika to the pot with the lardons and cook for 1 minute. (You can skip this stage, but searing the lardons does help to lock in the flavour and release the oil from the lardons.)

Put the carrot, celery and garlic in the pot of the slow cooker along with the lardons and paprika. Add the tomato purée, vinegar and sugar, then tip in the chopped tomatoes and butter beans with the rosemary. Stir well to mix everything together, then cover the pot with the lid.

Set the slow cooker to 'cook' mode, then turn it either to high and cook for 3 hours or to low and cook for 5 hours.

When ready to serve, season with salt and pepper to taste and grate over a little Parmesan, if you like.

RATATOUILLE

SERVES 4

One of the easiest and most delicious ways to get your five-a-day, a ratatouille is such a useful recipe to have in your back pocket. Served with couscous, it's substantial enough to be a main meal, or it makes a tasty side dish to accompany sausages, chops, chicken, pretty much anything... If you have the time, the 10 minutes of frying at the very start helps to caramelise the onion, then you can leave it to do its thing in the slow cooker.

⏲ Cooking time: 3 hours 10 minutes on high; 6 hours 10 minutes on low

🍳 Preparation time: 10 minutes

♥ Calories: 262 kcals per serving (with couscous)

1 tablespoon olive oil

1 red onion, sliced

1 aubergine, cut into rough 2cm chunks

2 peppers (any colour – I use red and yellow), cut into rough 2cm chunks

2 courgettes, halved lengthways and sliced into rough 1cm slices

5 tomatoes (about 450g), cut into rough chunks

2 tablespoons tomato purée

4 garlic cloves, crushed

1 tablespoon red wine vinegar

1 teaspoon sugar

3 thyme sprigs, leaves picked

200g couscous

Optional – If it has one, set the slow cooker to 'fry' mode (or use a frying pan over a medium heat for this stage). Add the olive oil to the pot of the slow cooker or frying pan and warm for a minute, then add the onion and cook for 7 minutes. Next, add the aubergine, peppers and courgettes and cook for a further 3 minutes. (You can skip this stage, but frying the vegetables does help to kickstart the caramelisation process.)

Put the tomatoes, tomato purée, garlic, red wine vinegar, sugar and thyme in the pot of the slow cooker along with the onion, aubergine, peppers and courgettes. Season well with plenty of salt and pepper. Cover the pot with the lid.

Set the slow cooker to 'cook' mode, then turn it either to high and cook for 3 hours or to low and cook for 6 hours.

With 10 minutes of the cooking time left, prepare the couscous by placing it in a heatproof bowl and covering with 300ml boiling water (or follow the packet instructions). Cover the bowl with clingfilm and let sit for 10 minutes.

When ready to serve, fluff up the couscous with a fork and season with salt and pepper. Serve the ratatouille on top of the couscous.

COOK'S TIP

If you chop the veggies more finely, this ratatouille makes a great base for a pasta sauce which can then be eaten either hot or cold – in fact, it makes a great packed lunch.

BROCCOLI AND CHEDDAR SOUP

SERVES 4

If you have some broccoli to use up, this gorgeously creamy soup takes no effort at all. For a lunch for two, a really fun way to serve this soup is in a bread bowl made from a hollowed-out loaf, then all you need is two spoons! The inside of the loaf soaks up the soup and turns gorgeously soft. It's up to you how much of the bread you eat. Otherwise, ladle the soup into bowls and serve with slices of crusty bread or farmhouse rolls.

 Cooking time: 2 hours 30 minutes on high; 4 hours 30 minutes on low

 Preparation time: 5 minutes

Calories: 286 kcals per serving (without bread)

1 head of broccoli, chopped into small pieces

1 onion, diced

1 carrot, grated

1 teaspoon garlic paste

1 tablespoon butter

1 vegetable or chicken stock pot mixed with 500ml boiling water

400ml semi-skimmed milk

½ x 165g tub cream cheese (I use Philadelphia)

100g Cheddar, grated

30ml single cream (I use Elmlea)

Salt and freshly ground black pepper

Put the broccoli, onion, carrot, garlic paste and butter in the pot of the slow cooker, then season with ¼ teaspoon salt and ½ teaspoon pepper. Pour in the stock and milk, then cover the pot with the lid.

Set the slow cooker to 'cook' mode, then turn it either to high and cook for 2 hours or to low and cook for 4 hours.

Stir the cream cheese and grated Cheddar through the soup, then cook on high for a further 30 minutes.

When ready to serve, add a dash of cream and stir into the soup. Pour the soup into the bread bowl (see below) or ladle into deep soup bowls.

COOK'S TIP

To make the bread bowl, cut the top off a crusty cob or sourdough loaf, then scoop out the inside. If you prefer, you can brush the inner walls of the bread bowl with a little oil and then cook it in an air fryer until golden before filling with the soup.

VEGGIE LASAGNE SOUP

Because this versatile soup is ideal for using up lots of veggies, I often make it on a day when I'm clearing out the fridge. Halfway between a soup and a pasta dish, this is a bit like minestrone. The ricotta added on top at the end gives the whole dish a fresh creaminess.

Cooking time: 2 hours on high; 4 hours on low

Preparation time: 15 minutes

Calories: 315 kcals per serving

1 onion, diced

1 red onion, diced

2 carrots, diced

2 celery stalks, diced

2 courgettes, diced

1 red pepper, diced

1 teaspoon garlic paste

1 teaspoon dried oregano

1 teaspoon chilli flakes

1 teaspoon sugar

2 vegetable stock pots

1 x 500ml carton passata

250g ribbon-shaped pasta (I use mafalde or mafalde corta pasta, but you can use any thick ribbon shape, like tagliatelle)

80g mozzarella, grated

240g ricotta

Salt and freshly ground black pepper

Put the onions, carrot, celery, courgettes, pepper and garlic paste in the pot of the slow cooker. Sprinkle in the dried oregano, chilli flakes and sugar, then season with a pinch each of salt and pepper.

Add the stock pots to the pot, then pour in the passata. Fill the passata carton with water and pour that into the slow cooker – do this twice. Cover the pot with the lid.

Set the slow cooker to 'cook' mode, then either turn it to high and cook for 2 hours or turn it to low and cook for 4 hours.

With 1 hour of the cooking time left, add the pasta to the pot, stir well and replace the lid.

Once the pasta is cooked, stir the grated mozzarella through the soup, replace the lid and cook for a few minutes or until the cheese has melted.

When ready to serve, ladle the soup into deep bowls and add a dollop of ricotta on top of each bowl.

COOK'S TIP

I love the frilled edge of the mafalde pasta, but you can use any flat ribbon shape you have to hand. You could even break up a regular lasagne sheet and use the shards instead.

SHAKSHUKA

This dish of eggs cooked in a mildly spiced tomato sauce has become a staple on brunch menus. Because they're baked in the sauce, the eggs end up with soft yolks with slightly jammy edges. I use a carton of 6 eggs to serve 3 people, but depending on how many you have to feed, you could use 8 eggs or 4 eggs – just add 200g more or less chopped tomatoes. Serve the shakshuka with toasted pitta or warmed flatbreads.

 Cooking time: 2 hours 25 minutes on high; 4 hours 25 minutes on low

 Preparation time: 5 minutes

 Calories: 244 kcals per serving (without flatbread)

For the sauce

1 red onion, chopped

1 red pepper, diced

1 garlic clove, crushed

1 tablespoon harissa paste (optional)

2 tablespoons tomato purée

1 teaspoon sugar

2 x 400g tins chopped tomatoes

Salt and freshly ground black pepper

To serve

6 medium eggs

2 tablespoons natural yoghurt

5g coriander, chopped

Put all the ingredients for the sauce in the pot of the slow cooker.

Set the slow cooker to 'cook' mode, then turn it either to high and cook for 2 hours (removing the lid for the final 30 minutes) or to low and cook for 4 hours (removing the lid for final 1 hour).

Make 6 wells in the tomato sauce and break an egg into each one. Season with salt and pepper, then cover the pot with the lid and cook for 20–25 minutes on high, or until the eggs are set.

Spoon the sauce into shallow bowls, placing two eggs on top of each bowlful. Drizzle over the yoghurt and scatter on some coriander, if you like.

COOK'S TIP

The harissa in the sauce gives a smoky, sweet warmth to the dish, but feel free to it leave out, if you prefer.

CREAMY TOMATO SOUP

SERVES
6

A steaming bowl of tomato soup may just be the ultimate comfort food on a chilly day. My version has an extra freshness compared to the tinned kind as it is made from a mix of fresh tomatoes – it's great for using up any tomatoes that are slightly passed their best, so throw those in too. I love to serve this soup with a chunk of crusty bread or even a cheese toastie for dunking.

 Cooking time: 4 hours 10 minutes on high; 8 hours 10 minutes on low

 Preparation time: 10 minutes

 Calories: 144 kcals per serving (without bread or cheese toastie)

1 teaspoon olive oil

1 onion, roughly chopped

2 celery stalks, roughly chopped

1.4kg ripe tomatoes (I use a mixture of large vine and cherry tomatoes), halved or quartered

2 tablespoons tomato purée

2 tablespoons tomato ketchup

1 teaspoon garlic granules

1 teaspoon celery salt

200ml hot vegetable or chicken stock

100ml double cream (I use Elmlea), plus extra to serve

Optional – If it has one, set the slow cooker to 'fry' mode (or use a frying pan over a medium heat for this stage). Add the olive oil to the pot of the slow cooker or frying pan, then toss in the chopped onion and celery and cook for 6–7 minutes, or until softened. (You can skip this stage, but frying the onion does help to kickstart the caramelisation process.)

Tumble the tomatoes into the pot of the slow cooker along with the onion and celery. Squeeze in the tomato purée and tomato ketchup, then stir in the garlic granules and celery salt. Pour in the stock. Cover the pot with the lid.

Set the slow cooker to 'cook' mode, then turn it either to high and cook for 4 hours or to low and cook for 8 hours.

Once cooked, using a handheld stick blender, blitz the soup until smooth. Stir through the cream.

When ready to serve, ladle the soup into deep bowls and serve with an extra drizzle of cream on top.

COOK'S TIP

I love having a batch of this comforting soup in the freezer, which keeps for months. Freeze the soup in individual portions ready to thaw and reheat until piping hot.

GARLIC MUSHROOMS WITH BABY POTATOES

These garlic mushrooms are so satisfying that I eat them straight up from a bowl. The added baby potatoes makes it more of a complete meal, but it also makes a terrific side dish to accompany roast chicken or beef. You can also jazz things up by spooning the mushrooms and potatoes into a heatproof dish, scattering over some grated cheese and popping it under the grill.

Cooking time: 2 hours 5 minutes on high; 4 hours 5 minutes on low

Preparation time: 5 minutes

Calories: 330 kcals per serving

25g salted butter

4 garlic cloves, crushed

650g chestnut mushrooms (left whole)

700g baby potatoes, any larger ones cut in half

1 vegetable stock pot mixed with 500ml boiling water

1 teaspoon dried parsley

3 teaspoons cornflour

120ml double cream (I use Elmlea)

1 tablespoon chopped parsley

Salt and freshly ground black pepper

Preheat the slow cooker, then add the butter and garlic to the pot. Heat briefly until the garlic smells fragrant.

Add the mushrooms and potatoes to the pot of the slow cooker. Pour over the hot stock and scatter in the dried parsley. Season well with salt and pepper, then stir well to combine. Cover the pot with the lid.

Turn the slow cooker to 'cook' mode, then turn it either to high and cook for 2 hours or to low and cook for 4 hours.

Remove 2 tablespoons of the sauce and combine with the cornflour in a small bowl. Stir this cornflour mixture back into the sauce in the pot. Continue to cook, with the lid off, for a further 5 minutes.

When ready to serve, stir through the double cream and scatter over the chopped parsley.

STUFFED PEPPERS

**SERVES
2-4**

Stuffed peppers are so easy to throw together and yet really tasty. They're also a great way to use up any leftovers. Try halving the amount of couscous and then layer in some leftover chilli con carne or even curry. This recipe serves four as a light meal with a side salad, or for something more substantial, dish up two peppers per person.

⏲ Cooking time: 3 hours on high;
6 hours on low

🍲 Preparation time: 10 minutes

♡ Calories: 456 kcals per serving
(based on 2 peppers per serving)

4 peppers (any colour, about 180g each)

2 teaspoons harissa

175ml hot vegetable stock

½ red onion, finely chopped

100g cherry tomatoes, diced

100g couscous

½ tablespoon olive oil

5g parsley, roughly chopped

100g feta, diced

Salt and freshly ground black pepper

First, prepare the peppers. Carefully remove the stalks, then scoop out the seeds with a teaspoon. If needed, slightly trim the bases of the peppers to create a flat bottom so they stand upright – but make sure you don't cut through into the centre cavity of the pepper. Set aside.

Stir together the harissa and hot stock in a jug.

Put the onion, tomatoes and couscous in a heatproof bowl. Pour in the stock to cover the couscous and let sit for 5 minutes.

Add the olive oil and chopped parsley to the couscous, then fluff up the grains with a fork. Season with plenty of salt and pepper, then stir through the diced feta.

Spoon the couscous mixture into the peppers and arrange them in the slow cooker, making sure they stand upright. (You may need to lean the peppers against each other or use some foil to prop them up.) Cover the pot with the lid.

Set the slow cooker to 'cook' mode, then turn it either to high and cook for 3 hours or to low and cook for 6 hours, or until the peppers are soft.

COOK'S TIP

If you're serving up these stuffed peppers to vegetarians, make sure the feta is suitable. Most feta is vegetarian nowadays, but it's definitely worth checking.

CHAPTER 3

FAKEAWAYS

MADRAS-STYLE BEEF CURRY

SERVES 4

Beef shin is one of the cheaper cuts of meat that benefits from a long time in the slow cooker as it becomes more tender the longer it cooks. Let the appliance do all the hard work for you – simply pop the ingredients into the slow cooker before you head off to work, then you'll come home to a Friday-night curry ready to serve. Scoop up the curry with some naan bread and enjoy it melt in your mouth.

- Cooking time: 4 hours 20 minutes on high; 8 hours 20 minutes on low
- Preparation time: 10 minutes
- Calories: 396 kcals per serving (without rice or naan)

½ tablespoon sunflower oil

500g beef shin, cut into rough 2cm cubes

1 onion, chopped

4 garlic cloves, crushed

1 tablespoon ginger paste

½ x 280g jar Madras curry paste (about 140g)

2 tablespoons tomato purée

½ x 400g tin chopped tomatoes (about 200g)

250g vine tomatoes, chopped

½ beef stock pot

To serve

Sliced red chilli (optional)

Coriander leaves (optional)

Optional – If it has one, set the slow cooker to 'fry' mode (or use a frying pan on the hob for this stage). Add the sunflower oil to the pot of the slow cooker or frying pan, followed by the beef and cook for 7–8 minutes or until browned. You may need to do this in batches. (You can skip this stage, but searing the beef does seal the meat and lock in the flavour.) Transfer the beef to a bowl and set aside.

Put the onion in the pot of the slow cooker and cook on high for 7–8 minutes, or until softened.

Add the garlic, ginger paste, curry paste and tomato purée to the pot, then cook, while stirring, for 1 minute.

Add the beef to the pot, then add the chopped tomatoes, vine tomatoes and stock pot. Cover the pot with the lid.

Set the slow cooker to 'cook' mode, then turn it either to high and cook for 4 hours or to low and cook for 8 hours.

When ready to serve, garnish the curry with the red chilli slices and coriander leaves (if using).

COOK'S TIP

If you find a Madras curry a little too spicy, simply pick the curry paste for your favourite type, like korma or vindaloo.

CHUNKY BEEF CHILLI

This chilli has had an upgrade. Instead of using regular beef mince, it's made with chunks of extra-lean diced beef. After hours in the slow cooker, the beef becomes super tender from the low and slow cooking, making a rich and warming stew.

Cooking time: 4 hours 15 minutes on high; 8 hours 15 minutes on low

Preparation time: 10 minutes

Calories: 360 kcals per serving (without tortilla chips, tortilla wraps or rice)

500g extra-lean diced beef

1 tablespoon flour

½ tablespoon sunflower oil

1 onion, chopped

2 peppers (any colour), cut into rough 2cm cubes

3 garlic cloves, crushed

1½ tablespoons chipotle paste

1½ teaspoons ground cumin

3 tablespoons tomato purée

2 vine tomatoes (about 180g), diced

1 beef stock pot

Salt and freshly ground black pepper

To serve

Handful of chopped coriander (optional)

Your choice of tortilla chips, tortillas wraps or rice

Season the beef with salt and pepper, then toss the pieces in the flour.

Optional – If it has one, set the slow cooker to 'fry' mode (or use a frying pan on the hob for this stage). Add the sunflower oil to the pot of the slow cooker or frying pan, followed by the beef and cook for 7–8 minutes or until browned. You may need to do this in batches. (You can skip this stage, but searing the beef does help to lock in the flavour.) Transfer the beef to a bowl and set aside.

Put the onion and peppers in the pot of the slow cooker and cook on high for 4–5 minutes, or until softened.

Add the garlic, chipotle paste and ground cumin to the pot, then cook, while stirring, for a further 1 minute.

Add the beef to the pot, then add the tomato purée, diced vine tomatoes and stock pot. Cover the pot with the lid.

Set the slow cooker to 'cook' mode, then turn it either to high and cook for 4 hours or to low and cook for 8 hours.

When ready to serve, scatter over the chopped coriander (if using), then serve with tortilla chips, tortilla wraps or rice for scooping up the chilli.

BEEF CURRY WITH POTATOES AND PEANUTS

If you enjoy the taste of satay skewers with peanut sauce, then you'll love this Massaman-style curry. Mildly spiced with the flavours of coconut and peanuts, it's deliciously rich without being heavy. It is an all-in-one dish, with the potatoes cooking in the peanutty sauce, but if you want to then you could always add rice.

- Cooking time: 4 hours 5 minutes on high; 8 hours 5 minutes on low
- Preparation time: 10 minutes
- Calories: 591 kcals per serving (without rice)

650g beef shin, cut into rough 2cm chunks

1 tablespoon sunflower oil

1 onion, sliced

400g new potatoes, halved or quartered

1 red chilli, chopped (deseeded, if liked)

1 x 190g jar Massaman curry spice paste

1 tablespoon smooth peanut butter

1 x 400ml tin light coconut milk

30g salted peanuts, roughly chopped (plus a few extra to serve)

Salt and freshly ground black pepper

Season the beef with salt and pepper.

Optional – If it has one, set the slow cooker to 'fry' mode (or use a frying pan on the hob for this stage.) Add the sunflower oil to the pot of the slow cooker or frying pan, followed by the beef and cook for 4–5 minutes, or until it starts to take on some colour. (You can skip this stage, but searing the beef does help to lock in the flavour.)

Add the onion, new potatoes and red chilli to the pot, then stir in the curry paste and peanut butter. Pour in the coconut milk, then add the chopped peanuts and stir well to mix everything together. Cover the pot with the lid.

Set the slow cooker to 'cook' mode, then turn it either to high and cook for 4 hours or to low and cook for 8 hours.

When ready to serve, divide the curry between bowls and scatter over a few extra chopped peanuts.

BARBECUE PULLED PORK BUNS

This pulled pork is so amazingly moist and incredibly moreish, especially when piled into burger buns with a crunchy slaw. It makes quite a big batch, so it's great for when you're entertaining, but it also freezes really well. Try any leftovers stirred into a pasta bake or piled in jacket potatoes.

Cooking time: 4 hours 20 minutes on high; 8 hours 20 minutes on low

Preparation time: 15 minutes

Calories: 545 kcals per serving (with slaw and bun)

1 tablespoon plain flour

2 teaspoons smoked paprika

2 teaspoons cayenne pepper

2 teaspoons garlic granules

½ tablespoon sunflower oil

Around 1.6kg boneless pork shoulder, skin and fat removed, then cut into 6–8 pieces

1 onion, sliced

150g barbecue sauce

150ml zero-sugar tropical fruit drink (I use Tropical Crush)

2 tablespoons red wine vinegar

1 tablespoon soft brown sugar

10 sesame seed brioche burger buns, to serve

For the slaw

¼ Savoy cabbage, shredded

1 large carrot, grated

1 tablespoon light mayonnaise

Juice of 1 lemon

1 teaspoon mustard

Combine the flour, paprika, cayenne pepper and garlic granules in a small bowl, then sprinkle over the pork.

Optional – If it has one, set the slow cooker to 'fry' mode (or use a frying pan on the hob for this stage). Add the sunflower oil to the pot of the slow cooker or frying pan, followed by the pork and cook for 7–8 minutes, or until browned on all sides. You may need to do this in batches. (You can skip this stage, but searing the pork does help to lock in the flavour.)

Put the onion in the pot of the slow cooker, along with the pork and any remaining flour.

Combine the barbecue sauce, tropical fruit drink, red wine vinegar and brown sugar in a jug, then pour this barbecue sauce mixture over the pork. Cover the pot with the lid.

Set the slow cooker to 'cook' mode, then turn it either to high and cook for 4 hours or to low and cook for 8 hours.

Transfer the pork to a board, shred it with two forks and set aside in a bowl.

Bring the cooking liquid left in the pot of the slow cooker to the boil either in the slow cooker (if it has a 'boil' mode) or in a saucepan over the hob. Let the liquid bubble away for 7–8 minutes, or until reduced and thickened. Pour this sauce over the shredded pork and toss to coat all the meat.

When ready to serve, prepare the slaw by combining all the ingredients in a mixing bowl.

Split open the burger buns, spoon some of the slaw onto the bases of the buns and top with the pulled pork before replacing the bun lids.

PORK AND PEANUT NOODLES

SERVES 4

When we cooked these noodles to take the photograph you see here, as soon as the shot was taken, everyone tucked in. The whole of the shoot team called them 'banging'! Sweet, salty, spicy – they bring all the feels. Best of all, there is virtually no prep needed to make this dish. You're done in under five minutes. If you're keeping an eye on the calories, just go careful on the peanuts.

🏺 Cooking time: 3 hours 10 minutes on high; 6 hours 10 minutes on low

🍲 Preparation time: 5 minutes

♡ Calories: 474 kcals per serving

500g pork mince (5% fat)

1 onion, sliced

1 tablespoon flour

2 garlic cloves, crushed

2 tablespoons gochujang paste

2 tablespoons smooth peanut butter

3 tablespoons dark soy sauce

2 tablespoons rice vinegar

1 x 400ml tin light coconut milk

1 x 400g pack straight-to-wok egg noodles

To serve

20g salted peanuts, chopped

2 spring onions, sliced

Optional – If it has one, set the slow cooker to 'fry' mode (or use a frying pan on the hob for this stage). Add the pork mince to the pot of the slow cooker or frying pan and dry fry for 4 minutes, or until lightly browned. (You can skip this stage, but searing the pork mince does lock in the flavour.)

Put the onion and flour in the pot of the slow cooker along with the pork mince, then cook on high for 1 minute.

Add the garlic, gochujang paste and peanut butter to the pot, followed by the soy sauce, vinegar and coconut milk, then stir to combine. Cover the pot with the lid.

Set the slow cooker to 'cook' mode, then turn it either to high and cook for 3 hours or to low and cook for 6 hours.

When ready to serve, stir the egg noodles through the pork mixture in the slow cooker for 5 minutes to warm them through. Serve the noodles topped with the chopped peanuts and sliced spring onions.

CHINESE-STYLE PORK SPARE RIBS

SERVES
4

Pork ribs cooked in the slow cooker are really succulent, so you absolutely have to try this recipe. The next time you're putting together a Saturday-night fakeaway meal, make sure you serve up these gorgeously sticky ribs alongside your other favourite Chinese-inspired dishes. There's just one thing I haven't listed in what you need below... that's plenty of paper napkins!

Cooking time: 4 hours 10 minutes on high; 8 hours 10 minutes on low

Preparation time: 5 minutes

Calories: 590 kcals per serving

800g pork ribs

100ml dark soy sauce

75ml hoisin sauce

70ml sweet chilli sauce

50g dark muscovado sugar

1 tablespoon garlic and ginger paste

2 teaspoons Chinese five spice powder

3 teaspoons cornflour

1 teaspoon toasted sesame seeds

Place the ribs in the slow cooker. If possible, arrange them in a single layer over the base of the pot.

Combine the soy sauce, hoisin sauce, sweet chilli sauce, sugar, garlic and ginger paste and five spice powder in a bowl, then pour the sauce mixture over the ribs. Cover the pot with the lid.

Set the slow cooker to 'cook' mode, then turn it either to high and cook for 4 hours or to low and cook for 8 hours.

Remove 2 tablespoons of the sauce and combine with the cornflour in a small bowl to make a smooth paste. Stir this cornflour paste back into the sauce in the pot. Continue to cook, with the lid off, for a further 10 minutes.

When ready to serve, scatter the sesame seeds over the spare ribs.

COOK'S TIP

For an even thicker sauce, once the ribs are cooked, pour the sauce into a saucepan, bring to the boil and cook until reduced, thick and glossy.

PORK BELLY RAMEN

SERVES 4

Pork belly cooked in chicken stock in the slow cooker makes an amazingly rich broth, which feels like it's really doing you good. I always add a soft-boiled egg to my bowl, but you can add whichever garnishes you fancy. And you can always adjust the spice level with more or less chilli oil.

- Cooking time: 3 hours 10 minutes
- Preparation time: 10 minutes
- Calories: 592 kcals per serving (without optional garnishes)

1 tablespoon vegetable oil

4 pork belly strips (about 600g)

250g shiitake mushrooms

4 tablespoons white miso paste

1 tablespoon garlic paste

1 tablespoon ginger paste

1 tablespoon dark soy sauce

2.5 litres hot chicken stock

Pinch of chilli flakes

Good grinding of black pepper

200g ramen noodles

2 pak choi, quartered

To serve (optional)

2 spring onions, thinly sliced

4 soft-boiled eggs, halved

Chilli oil

Toasted sesame seeds

Optional – If it has one, set the slow cooker to 'fry' mode (or use a non-stick frying pan over a medium–high heat for this stage). Heat the vegetable oil then cook the pork belly strips for 8–10 minutes or until golden brown on each side. (You can skip this stage, but searing the pork does help to lock in the flavour.) Transfer the pork to a plate and set aside.

Put the mushrooms in the pot of the slow cooker and cook on high for 5 minutes, then add the pork belly strips to the pot with the mushrooms.

Combine the miso paste, garlic paste, ginger paste, soy sauce and a splash of the stock in a jug. Spoon this miso mixture over the mushrooms and pork, then pour in the remaining stock.

Sprinkle in the chilli flakes and ground black pepper. Cover the pot with the lid.

Set the slow cooker to 'cook' mode and turn it to high and cook for 2 hours 30 minutes. After this time, remove the pork belly strips.

Add a splash of oil to a non-stick pan and fry the pork strips over a high heat for 5 minutes or until golden brown on each side. Transfer to a chopping board and slice the pork into chunks.

Add the noodles and pak choi to the broth in the slow cooker and cook for 15–20 minutes or until the noodles are cooked through.

When ready to serve, divide the pork, noodles and broth between four deep bowls. Finish with the sliced spring onions, soft-boiled eggs, toasted sesame seeds and chilli oil (if using).

LAMB ROGAN JOSH

SERVES 4

Low and slow cooking allows lamb to become really tender and juicy, which makes it perfect for soaking up all those curry flavours. I love a good curry. This one doesn't use many ingredients, so you can pop it on even when you're in a rush and still get to enjoy a curry packed with flavour! I like to serve it alongside plain basmati rice to cool down the warming spices.

- Cooking time: 8 hours 10 minutes on low
- Preparation time: 10 minutes
- Calories: 293 kcals per serving (without rice or naan)

500g diced lamb

1 tablespoon flour

1 onion, diced

1 red chilli, diced (optional)

2 tablespoons Rogan Josh spice paste

1 teaspoon garlic paste

1 x 400g tin chopped tomatoes

Salt and freshly ground black pepper

Handful of chopped coriander, to serve (optional)

Season the lamb with salt and pepper, then toss it in the flour.

Optional – If it has one, set the slow cooker to 'fry' mode (or alternatively use a frying pan on the hob for this stage). Add the olive oil to the pot of the slow cooker or frying pan, followed by the lamb and cook for 7–8 minutes or until browned – you may need to do this in batches. (You can skip this stage, but searing the lamb does help to lock in the flavour.)

Put the onion and red chilli (if using) in the pot of the slow cooker along with the lamb, then stir in the spice paste and garlic paste. Next, pour in the chopped tomatoes. Fill the empty tin half full with water, swirl it around and add that to the pot and give everything a good stir. Cover the pot with the lid.

Set the slow cooker to 'cook' mode, then turn it to low and cook for 8 hours, or until the lamb easily falls apart. If you prefer a drier curry, put a clean tea towel under the lid of the slow cooker to absorb some of the steam and allow the sauce to thicken up. Alternatively, leave the lid slightly ajar so that some of the steam can escape.

When ready to serve, scatter the curry with the chopped coriander (if using).

COOK'S TIP

You can use up any leftovers by filling wraps or naans with the lamb curry, some mango chutney and a little mint raita.

SATAY CHICKEN CURRY NOODLES

Let's face it, peanut butter makes everything delicious. It's definitely a storecupboard ingredient that I can't live without. The same goes for coconut milk. Rather than cooking with stock in the slow cooker, using coconut milk gives this noodle dish a creamy richness. Then if you want a little bit more heat, stir through some extra sweet chilli sauce at the very end just before serving.

Cooking time: 3 hours on high; 5 hours 30 minutes on low

Preparation time: 5 minutes

Calories: 522 kcals per serving

2 large skinless chicken breasts (about 350g)

1 onion, chopped

3 garlic cloves, crushed

1 tablespoon ginger paste

3 tablespoons smooth peanut butter

3 tablespoons dark soy sauce

2 tablespoons sweet chilli sauce

1 tablespoon medium curry powder

1 x 400ml tin light coconut milk

½ x 226g pack dried medium egg noodles (about 110g)

Juice of 1 lime

Salt and freshly ground black pepper

To serve

2 spring onions, sliced

1 teaspoon toasted sesame seeds

Lime wedges, for squeezing over

Season the chicken breasts with salt and pepper, then put them in the pot of the slow cooker.

Add the onion, garlic, ginger paste, peanut butter, soy sauce, chilli sauce and curry powder. Pour in the coconut milk and stir to combine. Cover the pot with the lid.

Set the slow cooker to 'cook' mode, then turn it either to high and cook for 2 hours 30 minutes or to low and cook for 5 hours.

Next, add the dried noodles to the pot along with 75ml water. Make sure the noodles are submerged in the cooking liquid, then cook on high for a further 30 minutes.

When ready to serve, stir the lime juice through the noodles. As you stir, the chicken should easily shred.

Divide the noodles and chicken between three deep bowls, then top with the sliced spring onions and sesame seeds. Serve with a few extra lime wedges for squeezing over.

BUTTER CHICKEN

This creamy chicken curry is a family favourite! If you think butter chicken is a hassle to make, do try this recipe. The slow cooker takes away all the fuss, leaving you with a comforting dinner that's incredibly tasty. Butter chicken absolutely must be served with rice and naan to mop up that deliciously rich sauce – sometimes I make a cheesy naan for extra indulgence!

Cooking time: 4 hours 10 minutes on high; 8 hours 10 minutes on low

Preparation time: 10 minutes, plus marinating

Calories: 402 kcals per serving (without rice or naan)

4 skinless chicken breasts (about 600g), cut into bite-sized chunks

1 onion, diced

50g unsalted butter

2 tablespoons tomato purée

1 teaspoon sugar

1 x 500ml carton passata

60ml double cream (I use Elmlea)

Handful of chopped parsley or coriander (optional)

Salt and freshly ground black pepper

For the marinade

2 tablespoons Greek-style yoghurt

2 teaspoons garlic paste

1 teaspoon ginger paste

1–2 teaspoons chilli powder (depending on how spicy you like it)

3 teaspoons garam masala

3 teaspoons ground turmeric

1 teaspoon ground cumin

First, marinate the chicken. In a shallow bowl, combine the yoghurt, garlic paste, ginger paste, and 1 teaspoon each of the chilli powder, garam masala, turmeric and cumin. Season with salt and pepper, then stir well to mix everything together.

Add the chicken to the bowl with the marinade, stirring to make sure each piece is evenly coated. Leave to marinate in the fridge for at least 1 hour or preferably overnight.

When ready to cook, take the chicken out of the fridge and transfer it to the pot of the slow cooker, along with any marinade from the bowl. Add the onion, butter, tomato purée, sugar and the remaining chilli powder (if using), garam masala, turmeric and cumin. Pour in the passata, then stir to mix well. Cover the pot with the lid.

Set the slow cooker to 'cook' mode, then turn it either to high and cook for 4 hours or to low and cook for 8 hours.

Next, stir in the cream, replace the lid, then cook for a further 10 minutes.

When ready to serve, scatter some chopped parsley or coriander over the curry, if you like.

HONEY GARLIC CHICKEN

SERVES 4

This is another of my favourite Chinese takeaway-style dishes. Chicken thighs have a really good flavour, especially when slow cooked. If you have time, marinate the chicken for up to an hour to infuse the meat with all those delicious salty, sweet and spicy tastes. You can serve this chicken with rice or noodles along with your choice of steamed green veggies – I like Tenderstem broccoli.

⏲ Cooking time: 3 hours on high; 5 hours 30 minutes on low

⏲ Preparation time: 10 minutes

♡ Calories: 511 kcals (without rice, noodles or veg)

1kg boneless, skinless chicken thighs

100ml hot chicken stock

1 tablespoon cornflour

1 tablespoon toasted sesame seeds

1 spring onion, thinly sliced

For the marinade

5 tablespoons tomato purée

2 tablespoons garlic paste

4 tablespoons dark soy sauce

4 tablespoons honey

2 tablespoons rice vinegar

½ teaspoon chilli flakes (optional)

Salt and freshly ground black pepper

First, marinate the chicken. In a shallow bowl, whisk together the tomato purée, garlic paste, soy sauce, honey, vinegar and chilli flakes (if using). Season with salt and pepper, then stir well to mix everything together.

Add the chicken to the bowl with the marinade, stirring to make sure each piece is evenly coated. Leave to marinate in the fridge for up to 1 hour, if you have time.

When ready to cook, take the chicken out of the fridge and transfer it to the pot of the slow cooker, along with any marinade from the bowl. Pour in the chicken stock, then stir to mix well. Cover the pot with the lid.

Set the slow cooker to 'cook' mode, then turn it either to high and cook for 2 hours 30 minutes or to low and cook for 5 hours.

Remove 2 tablespoons of the sauce and combine with the cornflour in a small bowl to make a smooth paste. Stir this cornflour paste back into the sauce in the pot. Continue to cook on high, with the lid off, for a further 30 minutes or until the sauce has reduced. Season to taste.

When ready to serve, scatter over the sesame seeds and sliced spring onions.

THAI GREEN CHICKEN CURRY

Thai curry sauce is naturally thinner than the spice pastes used for Indian-style curries, so there's lots of flavourful juices for the chicken to soak up while it's slow cooking – the moist meat pulls apart beautifully when you're ready to serve. You can add any veg you like to this curry; it's great for using up bits from the fridge. Always serve with sticky jasmine rice to soak up even more of the fragrant sauce.

⏱ Cooking time: 2 hours 15 minutes on high; 4 hours 30 minutes on low

⏲ Preparation time: 5 minutes

♡ Calories: 323 kcals per serving (with rice)

4 skinless chicken breasts (about 600g)

1 x 170g jar Thai green curry paste (I use Blue Dragon)

1 x 400ml tin light coconut milk

1 teaspoon garlic paste

½ teaspoon ginger paste

Pinch of dried red chilli flakes (optional)

1 x 250g packet mixed vegetables (I use carrots, broccoli, beans and baby corn, but you can use peppers and mangetout)

1 red chilli, sliced

To serve

1 x 250g pouch microwave jasmine rice

Pinch of black sesame seeds (optional)

Place the chicken breasts in the pot of the slow cooker, then spoon over the curry paste. Pour a little of the coconut milk into the curry paste jar, tighten the lid and give it a good shake to get every last bit of the paste from the jar into the slow cooker.

Pour the rest of the coconut milk over the chicken and stir in the garlic paste, ginger paste and chilli flakes (if using). Cover the pot with the lid.

Set the slow cooker to 'cook' mode, then turn it either to high and cook for 2 hours or to low and cook for 4 hours.

Lift the lid off the pot, break up the cooked chicken – it should fall apart quite easily – then add the mixed veg along with the sliced red chilli. Put the lid back on and cook on high for a further 15 minutes or on low for a further 30 minutes.

When ready to serve, cook the rice following the packet instructions. Pack the rice in a small bowl, place a larger serving bowl on top and the flip them over. Remove the small bowl to reveal a perfectly shaped dome of rice.

Spoon the chicken curry around the rice and sprinkle over a small pinch of black sesame seeds (if using).

COOK'S TIP

Rather than chicken breasts, you can also use boneless, skinless chicken thighs.

PERI-PERI PULLED CHICKEN

SERVES 3

If you're looking for an easy yet deliciously juicy pulled chicken recipe, this is the one for you! It's perfect for making during the weekend and then can be used up over the following busy days – stored in an airtight container, it keeps well in the fridge for up to 3 days. I like to use this peri-peri pulled chicken in salads, wraps, rolls and sandwiches.

⏲ Cooking time: 1 hour 30 minutes on high; 3 hours on low

🍳 Preparation time: 5 minutes

♡ Calories: 192 kcals per serving

3 skinless chicken breasts (about 450g)

3 tablespoons peri-peri marinade (I use Nando's Peri-Peri Hot Marinade)

1 teaspoon smoked paprika

Salt and freshly ground black pepper

Butterfly the chicken breasts. Put them in the pot of the slow cooker, then spread with the hot marinade, making sure the chicken is evenly coated. Sprinkle over the paprika, then season well with plenty of salt and pepper. Cover the pot with the lid.

Set the slow cooker to 'cook' mode, then turn it either to high and cook for 1 hour 30 minutes or to low and cook for 3 hours, or until the chicken is cooked through and the meat shreds easily.

CHICKEN RICE BAKE WITH CRISPY ONIONS

At the start of this recipe, it's well worth spending the 10 minutes needed to fry the onions to get them nice and soft. Mixed through the rice, the caramelised onions give a lovely sweetness that contrasts with the crispy onions scattered on top to serve. For the rice, I use a pouch of mixed wild and basmati rice that has a delicious nuttiness.

⌂ Cooking time: 3 hours 15 minutes on low

⏱ Preparation time: 10 minutes

♡ Calories: 527 kcals per serving

1 tablespoon sunflower oil

3 onions, thinly sliced

4 boneless, skinless chicken thighs, chopped into bite-sized chunks

70g your favourite spice paste (any type – I use katsu curry, korma or tikka)

1 x 250g pouch wild and basmati rice, soaked in boiling water then drained

500ml hot chicken stock

To serve

40g crispy onions

1 lemon, cut into wedges

Mango chutney or curry sauce (optional)

If it has one, set the slow cooker to 'fry' mode (or you can use a frying pan over a medium heat for this stage). Add the sunflower oil to the pot of the slow cooker or frying pan. Allow the oil to heat, then add the sliced onions and cook for 10 minutes or until softened and caramelised.

Add the chicken to the pot of the slow cooker along with the onions. Spoon in the spice paste, stir well and cook on high for 3 minutes.

Put the drained rice in the pot. Cook on high for 2 minutes, then pour in the hot stock. Cover the pot with the lid.

Set the slow cooker to 'cook' mode, then turn it to low and cook for 3 hours.

When ready to serve, divide the rice bake between four deep bowls or plates and scatter over the crispy onions. Add the lemon wedges for squeezing over. Add a spoonful or two of mango chutney or curry sauce, if you like.

SWEET AND SOUR CHICKEN

SERVES 4

Apart from a couple of fresh red and yellow peppers, you're likely to have everything else needed for this dish already in the cupboard or fridge. For that reason, it's a great dinner option when you don't want to go further than the corner shop. The pineapple chunks and juice make this dish lovely and sweet – it's a great one for enticing the kids to eat some veg and fruit!

🔔 Cooking time: 2 hours 40 minutes on high; 5 hours 10 minutes on low

🍽 Preparation time: 5 minutes

♡ Calories: 367 kcals per serving (with rice)

6 boneless, skinless chicken thighs (about 640g), chopped into bite-sized chunks

2 peppers (I use red and yellow), cut into rough 2cm cubes

1 onion, cut into rough 2cm chunks

2 garlic cloves, crushed

4 tablespoons white rice vinegar

2 tablespoons tomato purée

3 tablespoons tomato ketchup

2 tablespoons dark soy sauce

1 tablespoon sugar

1 x 425g tin pineapple chunks in juice

2 tablespoons cornflour

Steamed rice, to serve

Put the chicken in the pot of the slow cooker, then toss in the peppers, onion and garlic. Stir in the vinegar, tomato purée, tomato ketchup, soy sauce and sugar.

Strain the juice from the tin of pineapple chunks, setting aside the chunks for later. Pour the pineapple juice over the chicken in the pot. Cover the pot with the lid.

Set the slow cooker to 'cook' mode, then turn it either to high and cook for 2 hours 30 minutes or to low and cook for 5 hours.

Remove 3 tablespoons of the sauce and combine with the cornflour in a small bowl to make a smooth paste. Stir this cornflour paste back into the sauce in the pot. Continue to cook on high, with the lid off, for a further 10 minutes or until the sauce has reduced and thickened. Season to taste.

When ready to serve, spoon the sweet and sour chicken into bowls filled with steamed rice.

CHINESE CURRY CHICKEN NOODLES

SERVES 4

This is not a dish that you'll find on any Chinese restaurant menu. It has more chip shop vibes than Michelin stars, but it's so, so tasty! All the curry flavours combine in the slow cooker and then the noodles are added in for the last 30 minutes of the cooking time, making it a brilliant all-in-one dish.

Cooking time: 3 hours 10 minutes on high; 5 hours 40 minutes on low

Preparation time: 10 minutes

Calories: 488 kcals per serving

2 tablespoons vegetable oil

2 skinless chicken breasts (about 300g), cut into thin strips

½ teaspoon Chinese five spice powder

1 onion, sliced

2 peppers (I use red and yellow), thinly sliced

1 carrot, finely chopped

4 tablespoons katsu curry paste or Chinese curry paste (I use Goldfish Chinese Curry Sauce Concentrate)

550ml hot chicken stock

2 tablespoons dark soy sauce

250g dried egg noodles

150g frozen garden peas, defrosted in hot water

4 spring onions, thinly sliced

Lime wedges, for squeezing over

Optional – If it has one, set the slow cooker to 'fry' mode (or use a frying pan over a medium heat for this stage). Add the vegetable oil to the pot of the slow cooker or frying pan and allow it to heat, then add the chicken and cook for 5–7 minutes or until golden brown. (You can skip this stage, but searing the chicken does help to lock in the flavour.)

Sprinkle the Chinese five spice powder over the chicken in the pot of the slow cooker, then cook on high for 1 minute.

Add the onion, peppers and carrot to the pot. Spoon the curry paste over the chicken, then pour in 300ml of the hot stock and soy sauce. Cover the pot with the lid.

Set the slow cooker to 'cook' mode, then turn it either to high and cook for 2 hours 30 minutes or to low and cook for 5 hours.

Next, pour in the remaining stock and then add the noodles and peas. Cook on high, with the lid off, for a further 30 minutes, stirring everything well after 15 minutes.

When ready to serve, toss the noodles and chicken together and season with salt to taste. Scatter over the sliced spring onions and serve with lime wedges for squeezing over.

PERI-PERI SPICED RICE

SERVES 4

This flavour-packed rice dish is one of my go-to sides, but it also makes a really handy base for a meal – just add your choice of protein. The spicy, smoky and sweet peri-peri flavours pair well not only with the classic chicken but also with steak, salmon and even halloumi!

Cooking time: 45 minutes on high

Preparation time: 5 minutes

Calories: 214 kcals per serving

200g basmati rice

½ onion, diced

½ red pepper, diced

80g frozen garden peas, defrosted in hot water

½ teaspoon cayenne pepper

1½ teaspoons smoked paprika

1½ teaspoons ground turmeric

1 teaspoon peri-peri salt (or regular salt)

Pinch of black pepper

250ml hot chicken or vegetable stock

150ml passata

Rinse the rice under cold running water until the water runs clear.

Put the rinsed rice in the pot of the slow cooker along with all the other ingredients. Stir well to mix everything together, making sure all the grains of rice are submerged in the liquid. Cover the pot with the lid.

Set the slow cooker to 'cook' mode, then turn it to high and cook for 45 minutes.

When ready to serve, fluff up the rice with a fork.

VEGGIE CHOW MEIN

SERVES 4

This is a veggie-packed dinner that is really easy to throw together. It feels light, while also being really hearty. The veg are pretty interchangeable so you can mix it up – just make sure you add anything smaller (like the mangetout) towards the end of the cooking time so that they don't overcook.

Cooking time: 1 hour 10 minutes on high; 2 hours 10 minutes on low

Preparation time: 5 minutes

Calories: 411 kcals per serving

½ onion, sliced

130g baby corn, cut into 3, widthways

3 spring onions, cut into 4, widthways

2 peppers (any colour), thinly sliced

250g medium egg noodles (raw)

300ml hot vegetable stock

70ml dark soy sauce

1 tablespoon Shaoxing or sherry vinegar

4 tablespoons hoisin sauce

2 teaspoons sesame oil

200g mangetout

Put all the vegetables (excluding the mangetout) in the pot of the slow cooker, then nestle the noodles in the middle.

Combine the hot stock, soy sauce, vinegar, hoisin and sesame oil in a jug, then pour the mixture over the veggies and noodles in the pot. Cover the pot with the lid.

Set the slow cooker to 'cook' mode, then turn it to high and cook for 1 hour or turn it to low and cook for 2 hours.

Add the mangetout to the noodles along with 100ml boiling water. Stir well enough to really loosen up the noodles, then cook on high, with the lid off, for a further 10 minutes.

FAMILY FAVOURITES

BOLOGNESE SAUCE

An Italian-style Bolognese sauce is naturally suited to cooking in a slow cooker, as the longer it cooks for, the yummier it gets. According to an old Italian saying, these sauces should only 'blip' and not 'bubble', so the slow cooker is perfect for achieving this. The classic way to serve this meat sauce is as a spag bol, but for lots of other ideas see my tips below.

Cooking time: 4 hours 20 minutes on high; 8 hours 20 minutes on low

Preparation time: 5 minutes

Calories: 237 kcals per serving (without spaghetti)

750g beef mince (5% fat)

2 onions, finely diced

1 large carrot, finely diced

2 celery stalks, finely chopped

6 garlic cloves, crushed

6 thyme sprigs, leaves picked

1 teaspoon dried mixed herbs

3 tablespoons tomato purée

2 teaspoons sugar

1 x 500ml carton passata

125ml red wine

1 tablespoon red wine vinegar

1 beef stock pot

Salt and freshly ground black pepper

Season the beef mince with salt and pepper.

Optional – If it has one, set the slow cooker to 'fry' mode (or use a frying pan on the hob for this stage). Add the beef mince to the pot of the slow cooker or frying pan and, breaking it up with a wooden spoon, cook for 5 minutes or until lightly browned. (You can skip this stage, but searing the beef mince does help to lock in the flavour.)

Put all the remaining ingredients in the pot of the slow cooker along with the mince, then stir to combine. Cover the pot with the lid.

Set the slow cooker to 'cook' mode, then turn it either to high and cook for 4 hours or to low and cook for 8 hours. (If you need to, the Bolognese sauce can be left on low for up to 10 hours.)

When ready to serve, turn the slow cooker to high and cook, with the lid off, for a final 15 minutes to thicken up the sauce a little.

COOK'S TIP

This versatile recipe can make more than a spag bol. Use it as the meat layer of a lasagne, as the base of a macaroni cheese, loaded into jacket potatoes, draped over potato wedges or sealed in a toastie. It's also brilliant in my Stuffed Peppers (see page 70).

BEEF CANNELLONI

SERVES 4-6

This dish uses all same the components as a lasagne, however using cannelloni pasta tubes instead of sheets of pasta makes it so much easier to portion out. No more fighting over who gets the largest slice!

 Cooking time: 2 hours 30 minutes on high; 4 hours 30 minutes on low

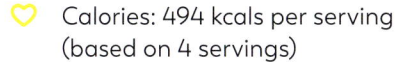 Preparation time: 15 minutes

Calories: 494 kcals per serving (based on 4 servings)

500g beef mince (5% fat)

½ onion, finely diced

2 garlic cloves, crushed

1 tablespoon tomato purée

1 tablespoon Worcestershire sauce

1 x 500ml carton passata with basil

175g cannelloni tubes (more or less, depending on the base of your slow cooker)

1 x 470g carton cheese sauce

30g Parmesan, grated

120g grated mozzarella and Cheddar mix

Salt and freshly ground black pepper

Season the beef mince with salt and pepper.

Optional – If it has one, set the slow cooker to 'fry' mode (or use a frying pan on the hob for this stage). Add the beef mince to the pot of the slow cooker or frying pan and, breaking it up with a wooden spoon, cook for 5 minutes or until lightly browned. (You can skip this stage, but searing the mince does help to lock in the flavour.) Transfer the beef mince to a bowl.

Add the diced onion, garlic, tomato purée and Worcestershire sauce to the bowl along with the beef mince. Pour in half of the passata, season well with salt and pepper, then stir to mix well.

Pour the remaining passata into the pot of the slow cooker to cover the base.

Fill the cannelloni tubes with the beef mixture, pushing it into the pasta tubes with a teaspoon or a cutlery handle, then lay them on top of the layer of tomato sauce.

Pour the cheese sauce over the cannelloni pasta tubes, making sure they are covered, then scatter over the grated Parmesan. Cover the pot with the lid.

Set the slow cooker to 'cook' mode, then turn it either to high and cook for 2 hours or to low and cook for 4 hours.

When ready to serve, scatter the grated mozzarella and Cheddar mix over the cannelloni and cook on high, with the lid off, for a final 20 minutes.

SLOPPY JOES

SERVES 6

These melt-in-the-mouth buns are filled with a thick, rich meat sauce, similar to a Bolognese, but sweetened with a little barbecue sauce. When you're having a get-together, they're a great thing to serve up to a crowd – prepare a selection of toppings and then leave your guests to add their own favourites. They do have the word 'sloppy' in their name, so remember to tuck in your napkin!

 Cooking time: 3 hours 15 minutes on high; 6 hours 15 minutes on low

 Preparation time: 5 minutes

 Calories: 386 kcals per serving (without toppings)

500g beef mince (5% fat)

1 onion, finely chopped

1 pepper (red or yellow), diced

250g chopped tomatoes

2 tablespoons barbecue sauce

6 white baps

100g Cheddar, grated, or 6 cheese slices

Salt and freshly ground black pepper

For the optional toppings

Yellow mustard

Tomato ketchup

Sliced gherkins

Sliced jalapeños

Crispy onions

Season the beef mince with salt and pepper.

Optional – If it has one, set the slow cooker to 'fry' mode (or use a frying pan on the hob for this stage). Add the beef mince to the pot of the slow cooker or frying pan and, breaking it up with a wooden spoon, cook for 5 minutes or until lightly browned. (You can skip this stage, but searing the beef mince does help to lock in the flavour.)

Put the chopped onion, diced pepper and chopped tomatoes in the pot of the slow cooker along with the mince. Stir in the barbecue sauce until well combined. Cover the pot with the lid.

Set the slow cooker to 'cook' mode, then turn it either to high and cook for 3 hours or to low and cook for 6 hours. (If you need to, the beef mixture can be left on low for up to 10 hours.)

When ready to serve, turn the slow cooker to high and cook, with the lid off, for a final 5–10 minutes to thicken up the sauce a little.

Split open the baps, then spoon the mince onto the bun bases. Top with a pile of grated cheese, or a cheese slice.

Encourage everyone to customise their Sloppy Joe with their choice of toppings, then squish the bun lid on top.

CHEESEBURGER PASTA

SERVES 4

Who says burgers have to be paired with bread? My all-time favourite carb is pasta, so I combined the elements of a burger in this creamy, cheesy pasta dish – it offers a delicious twist on an old favourite. It's simple, super tasty and has become a staple in my household.

 Cooking time: 1 hour 10 minutes on high

 Preparation time: 5 minutes

♡ Calories: 558 kcals per serving

500g beef mince (5% fat)

1 red onion, finely diced

1 teaspoon garlic paste

2 tablespoons tomato purée

2 tablespoons tomato ketchup

1 tablespoon English mustard

1 tablespoon Worcestershire sauce

1 teaspoon dried oregano

1 beef stock pot

300g conchiglie (or any other shell-shaped pasta)

300ml semi-skimmed milk

300ml boiling water

Salt and freshly ground black pepper

To serve

1 gherkin, sliced

30g Cheddar, grated

30g mozzarella, grated

30g red Leicester, grated

Season the beef mince with salt and pepper.

Optional – If it has one, set the slow cooker to 'fry' mode (or use a frying pan on the hob for this stage). Add the beef mince to the pot of the slow cooker or frying pan and, breaking it up with a wooden spoon, cook for 5 minutes or until lightly browned. (You can skip this stage, but searing the beef mince does help to lock in flavour.)

Put the rest of the ingredients in the pot of the slow cooker along with the mince, making sure the pasta is submerged in the liquid. Season with plenty of salt and pepper. Cover the pot with the lid.

Set the slow cooker to 'cook' mode, then turn it to high and cook for 1 hour.

When ready to serve, scatter over the sliced gherkin and all three grated cheeses. Put the lid back on the pot and cook on high for 5 minutes or until the cheese has melted.

CREAMY TOMATO MEATBALL PASTA

Browning off the meatballs at the very beginning of this recipe is well worth the time as it gets those extra meaty flavours into your pasta dish. Although meatballs are traditionally served on spaghetti, I prefer mine with a tube-shaped pasta, like rigatoni, as it holds lots of that delicious sauce.

Cooking time: 1 hour on high

Preparation time: 10 minutes

Calories: 522 kcals per serving

24 mini meatballs

A few pumps of spray oil

1 red onion, finely diced

1 red pepper, finely diced

100g button mushrooms, sliced

1 teaspoon lazy garlic from a jar (or 1 teaspoon garlic paste)

1 teaspoon lazy chilli from a jar (or ½ teaspoon chilli flakes)

1 teaspoon dried oregano

300g rigatoni (or any other tube-shaped pasta)

1 x 400ml tin chopped tomatoes

1 teaspoon sugar

1 tablespoon tomato purée

1 beef stock cube

45g light cream cheese (I use Philadelphia)

1 teaspoon chopped parsley, plus extra to serve

Salt and freshly ground black pepper

Season the meatballs with salt and pepper.

Optional – If it has one, set the slow cooker to 'cook' mode (or use a frying pan over a hob for this stage). Add the meatballs to the pot of the slow cooker or frying pan with a little spray oil and cook them on all sides until lightly browned. (You can skip this stage, but searing the meatballs does help to lock in the flavour.)

Put the red onion, red pepper and mushrooms in the pot of the slow cooker along with the meatballs. Next, add the garlic, chilli, dried oregano and a pinch each of salt and pepper. Tip in the rigatoni, stirring to mix everything well.

Pour in the chopped tomatoes. Fill the empty tin half full with water, swirl it around and add that to the pot and give everything a good stir. Mix in the sugar and tomato purée, then crumble the stock cube over the top. Cover the pot with the lid.

Set the slow cooker to 'cook' mode, then turn it to high and cook for 35–45 minutes, or until the pasta is cooked.

When ready to serve, spoon in the cream cheese, scatter in the parsley and stir to make sure everything is warmed through. Serve with a little more parsley sprinkled on top.

CHILLI BEEF PASTA BAKE

SERVES 6

Two classic dinners combine here in one amazing dish. Chilli with rice is delicious, but mixing it with a shell-shaped pasta means you can scoop up lots of cheesy chilli to make every bite a perfect one! Feel free to go wild when serving and add all of your usual favourite chilli toppings, like sour cream and guacamole.

 Cooking time: 1 hour 20 minutes on high; 2 hours 20 minutes on low

 Preparation time: 10 minutes

♡ Calories: 454 kcals per serving

500g beef mince (5% fat)

½ tablespoon sunflower oil

2 peppers (any colour – I use 1 red and 1 yellow), diced

2 tablespoons tomato purée

2 teaspoons ground cumin

1 tablespoon smoked paprika

1 teaspoon cayenne pepper

1 x 400g tin kidney beans in chilli sauce

1 x 500ml carton passata

1 beef stock pot mixed with 200ml boiling water

300g conchiglie (or any other shell-shaped pasta)

100g Cheddar, grated

2 tablespoons sliced jalapeños, from a jar (optional)

Salt and freshly ground black pepper

Season the beef mince with salt and pepper.

Optional – If it has one, set the slow cooker to 'fry' mode (or use a frying pan on the hob for this stage.) Add the sunflower oil to the pot of the slow cooker or frying pan, then add the mince and, breaking it up with a wooden spoon, cook for 5 minutes or until lightly browned. (You can skip this stage, but searing the mince does help to lock in the flavour.)

Put the diced peppers, tomato purée and ground spices in the pot of the slow cooker with the mince, then stir to combine.

Pour in the kidney beans and chilli sauce from the tin, passata and hot beef stock. Stir in the pasta, making sure it is submerged in the liquid. Cover the pot with the lid.

Set the slow cooker to 'cook' mode, then turn it either to high and cook for 1 hour or to low and cook for 2 hours.

When ready to serve, stir the pasta bake to mix everything together well, then top with the grated cheese and cook on high with the lid off for a final 15 minutes. Spoon into bowls and serve with the sliced jalapeños scattered over (if using).

PULLED BEEF BAGELS

With just a handful of ingredients, you can transform a plain joint of beef into a mouthwatering dinner that's bursting with flavour – it's sure to be loved by the whole family. Here I've served the pulled beef piled into bagels with gherkins and mustard, but it's so versatile. Why not try it loaded in a Yorkshire pudding wrap, which can be easily made in an air fryer. This is a recipe that can be eaten all year round, depending on how you serve it,

Cooking time: 8–12 hours on low (depending on the size of the beef joint)

Preparation time: 5 minutes

Calories: 209 kcals per serving (without bagel)

2kg beef roasting joint

1 x 440ml can stout (I use Guinness)

1 tablespoon Worcestershire sauce

1 teaspoon dried rosemary

1 teaspoon dried thyme

2 tablespoons gravy granules

Salt and freshly ground black pepper

To serve (optional)

Bagels, toasted

Sliced gherkins

Yellow mustard

Put the beef roasting joint in the pot of the slow cooker and season with salt and pepper. Pour over the stout and Worcestershire sauce, then sprinkle on the dried herbs. Cover the pot with the lid.

Set the slow cooker to 'cook' mode, turn it to low and cook for 8–12 hours. (I often cook mine overnight.)

Once cooked, use two forks to pull the meat apart. Leave the shredded beef in the pot to soak up the cooking juices.

When ready to serve, stir the gravy granules into the cooking juices in the pot and mix well to thicken.

Serve the pulled beef loaded into toasted bagels with slices of gherkin and a squirt of yellow mustard.

COOK'S TIP

Feel free to replace the stout with the same quantity of dark ale or bitter. If you prefer the dish to be alcohol free, you can always use beef stock instead.

CREAMY PERI-PERI CHICKEN PASTA

SERVES 4

This peri-peri pasta really packs a punch! The tangy, spicy flavours of peri-peri mixed with the creaminess of the cheese perfectly compliment the pasta here – it's a guaranteed crowd pleaser! You can use whichever type of peri-peri rub you prefer, depending on how spicy you like it.

 Cooking time: 2 hours 30 minutes on high; 4 hours 30 minutes on low

 Preparation time: 10 minutes

Calories: 596 kcals per serving

500g skinless chicken breasts, diced

1 onion, sliced

1 pepper (any colour – I use red and yellow), sliced

1 teaspoon garlic paste

1 tablespoon tomato purée

Pinch of chilli flakes

1 teaspoon smoked paprika

1 x 25g sachet peri-peri rub (I use Nando's medium)

1 chicken stock pot mixed with 300ml boiling water

300g farfalle (or any other bow-shaped pasta)

300ml semi-skimmed milk

80g light cream cheese (I use Philadelphia)

1 tablespoon peri-peri marinade (I use Nando's medium)

100g light Cheddar, grated

Salt and freshly ground black pepper

Put the chicken, onion, pepper, garlic paste and tomato purée in the pot of the slow cooker, then season with a pinch each of salt and pepper. Sprinkle over the chilli flakes, smoked paprika and sachet of peri-peri rub, then pour in the hot stock. Cover the pot with the lid.

Set the slow cooker to 'cook' mode, then turn it either to high and cook for 2 hours or to low and cook for 4 hours.

Add the pasta to the pot, then pour in the milk. Stir in the cream cheese and peri-peri marinade. Replace the lid on the pot, then cook for 30 minutes or until the pasta is cooked.

When ready to serve, scatter over the grated cheese and cook, with the lid on, until the cheese has melted.

POLLO PICANTE

SERVES 4

This is one of my favourite restaurant dishes that I just had to recreate at home. It's surprisingly easy. The smokiness from the harissa paste really enhances the flavours, but if you prefer less spice, reduce the quantity of harissa – you'll still get to enjoy all the delicious taste but with slightly less heat!

Cooking time: 1 hour 5 minutes on high; 2 hours 5 minutes on low

Preparation time: 10 minutes

Calories: 511 kcals per serving

2 large skinless chicken breasts, butterflied (about 350g)

½ teaspoon cayenne pepper

1 teaspoon smoked paprika

2–3 teaspoons harissa paste (depending on how spicy you like it)

600ml boiling water

360g casarecce (or any other scroll-shaped pasta), rinsed under boiling water

400g cherry tomatoes, halved

200g baby spinach

120ml single cream (I use Elmlea)

1 red chilli, sliced

Put the butterflied chicken breasts on a plate and rub them with the cayenne pepper and smoked paprika. Season well with salt and pepper.

In a jug, mix the harissa paste with the boiling water.

Put the rinsed pasta and cherry tomatoes in the pot of the slow cooker. Pour over the harissa water, then nestle the chicken breasts on top. Cover the pot with the lid.

Set the slow cooker to 'cook' mode, then turn it either to high and cook for 1 hour or to low and cook for 2 hours.

Carefully lift the chicken out of the slow cooker and place on a board.

Stir the spinach into the pot and cook, with the lid off, for about 3 minutes or until the spinach has wilted.

Meanwhile, slice the chicken breasts into thin strips.

Stir the cream into the pasta, then return the sliced chicken to the pot and stir to mix everything together. Test for the spice level and add more harissa if you want it more picante! Season with salt and pepper, if needed.

Divide the pasta between deep bowls and scatter over the sliced chilli to finish.

ENCHILADA BAKE

Enchiladas are so delicious, but sometimes I don't have the time or energy for all that stuffing, rolling and wrapping, which can be a bit of a fuss. This slow cooker method takes away the hassle of wrapping enchiladas, but keeps all the delicious familiar flavours we know and love!

Cooking time: 4 hours 15 minutes on high; 8 hours 15 minutes on low

Preparation time: 10 minutes

Calories: 577 kcals per serving (without optional toppings)

500g beef mince (5% fat)

1 beef stock pot or cube

1 onion, diced

1 red pepper, diced

2 tablespoons tomato purée

2 teaspoons ground cumin

2 teaspoons smoked paprika

1 teaspoon cayenne pepper

1 teaspoon dried oregano

1 x 400g tin kidney beans, drained and rinsed

1 x 500ml carton passata

8 mini tortillas, cut into strips

150g mozzarella, grated

Salt and freshly ground black pepper

For the optional toppings

Sliced red chilli

Sliced spring onions

Sliced jalapeños from a jar

Soured cream

Optional – If it has one, set the slow cooker to 'fry' mode (or use a frying pan on a hob for this stage). Put the beef mince in the pot of the slow cooker or frying pan with the stock pot or cube and cook for 7–8 minutes or until lightly browned. (You can skip this stage, but searing the mince does help to lock in flavour.)

Put the onion, pepper, tomato purée, cumin, paprika, cayenne pepper and dried oregano in the pot of the slow cooker along with the mince and stock pot or cube. Season with a pinch each of salt and pepper.

Tip the kidney beans and the passata into the pot. Fill the empty carton half full with water, swirl it around and add that to the pot and give everything a good stir. Cover the pot with the lid.

Set the slow cooker to 'cook' mode, then turn it either to high and cook for 4 hours or to low and cook for 8 hours.

When ready to serve, add the tortilla strips to the pot, stir, replace the lid and cook for a further 15 minutes.

With 5 minutes of the cooking time left, scatter the grated mozzarella over the top and cook with the lid on to melt the cheese.

When ready to serve, spoon the enchilada bake into bowls and add any additional toppings that you fancy.

CHICKEN FAJITAS

SERVES 4

A jar or sachet of fajita seasoning is something I always keep in my kitchen cupboards as it's an easy way to prepare a tasty fajita filling. When I crave a Tex-Mex fix, this slow-cooked chicken fajita never fails to hit the spot.

 Cooking time: 2 hours on high; 4 hours on low

 Preparation time: 5 minutes

 Calories: 406 kcals per serving

1 red onion, sliced

1 red pepper, cut into strips

1 yellow pepper, cut into strips

2 skinless chicken breasts (about 300g)

4½ teaspoons fajita seasoning

2 tablespoons tomato purée

50ml hot water

100g tomato salsa

To serve

4 tortilla wraps

50g Cheddar, grated

4 tablespoons soured cream

10g coriander leaves

Put the onion and peppers in the pot of the slow cooker, covering the base. Nestle the chicken breasts in between the veggies, then sprinkle over 3 teaspoons of the fajita seasoning.

In a jug, mix the tomato purée with the hot water, then pour it over the chicken and veg. Cover the pot with the lid.

Set the slow cooker to 'cook' mode, then turn it either to high and cook for 2 hours or to low and cook for 4 hours.

Carefully lift the chicken out of the slow cooker, place it on a board and slice into strips.

Using a ladle, spoon any excess liquid out of the slow cooker and discard. Return the chicken strips to the pot, sprinkle in the remaining fajita seasoning and stir through the tomato salsa. Make sure everything is warmed through.

When ready to serve, spoon the chicken fajita filling onto the centre of the tortilla wraps, then scatter over the grated cheese, soured cream and coriander leaves.

TUSCAN-STYLE CHICKEN ORZO

The intense summer flavours of sundried tomatoes and oregano in this easy pasta dish will instantly transport you straight to Italy. I love using orzo, a pasta shaped like small grains of rice, as it has a lovely velvety texture. This slow-cooker dish is a definite crowd pleaser.

Cooking time: 1 hour 25 minutes on high; 2 hours 45 minutes on low

Preparation time: 5 minutes

Calories: 514 kcals per serving

120g cream cheese (I use Philadelphia)

2 garlic cloves, crushed

2 teaspoons sweet smoked paprika

2 teaspoons dried oregano

375ml hot chicken stock

4 boneless, skinless chicken thighs, chopped into bite-sized chunks

250g orzo

75g sundried tomatoes, chopped

150g baby spinach

40g Parmesan, grated, plus extra to serve

Salt and freshly ground black pepper

In a jug, mix the cream cheese, garlic, paprika and oregano with the stock.

Put the chicken, orzo and sundried tomatoes in the pot of the slow cooker, covering the base. Pour over the cream cheese mixture, season with salt and pepper, then stir to combine. Cover the pot with the lid.

Set the slow cooker to 'cook' mode, then turn it either to high and cook for 1 hour 20 minutes or to low and cook for 2 hours 40 minutes.

Stir the spinach and grated Parmesan into the pot along with an extra 50–75ml water (to reach your desired consistency) and cook, with the lid off, for about 3 minutes or until the spinach has wilted.

Spoon the orzo into deep bowls and finish with a little extra Parmesan grated over the top, if you like.

CRUNCHY BEEF CHILLI RICE BAKE

SERVES 6

This super-simple, one-pot meal is great for meal prep – it tastes even better the day after it's made once the rice has absorbed all the flavours! If you're preparing it in advance, save the crunchy tortilla chip topping until you're ready to serve.

 Cooking time: 4 hours on high

 Preparation time: 5 minutes

♡ Calories: 489 kcals per serving

500g beef mince (5% fat)

1 onion, diced

2 peppers (I use red and green), diced

1 tablespoon garlic paste

2 tablespoons tomato purée

1 teaspoon cayenne pepper

1 teaspoon smoked paprika

1 teaspoon ground cumin

1 teaspoon dried oregano

1 x 400g tin chopped tomatoes

1 tablespoon Worcestershire sauce

350g long-grain rice, soaked in boiling water for 5 minutes, drained and rinsed

1 beef stock pot mixed with 400ml boiling water

150g grated red Leicester, Cheddar and mozzarella mix

Handful of sliced jalapeños from a jar

Salt and freshly ground black pepper

For the optional toppings

30g chilli tortilla chips (I use Doritos)

Tomato salsa

Guacamole

Soured cream

Optional – If it has one, set the slow cooker to 'fry' mode (or use a frying pan on a hob for this stage). Add the beef mince to the pot of the slow cooker or frying pan and cook for 7–8 minutes or until browned. (You can skip this stage, but searing the mince does help to lock in the flavour.)

Put the onion, peppers, garlic paste, tomato purée, ground spices and dried oregano in the pot of the slow cooker along with the beef mince. Pour in the chopped tomatoes, then season with the Worcestershire sauce and a pinch each of salt and pepper. Stir well to mix everything together. Cover the pot with the lid.

Set the slow cooker to 'cook' mode, then turn it to high and cook for 3 hours.

Next, add the rice and beef stock, then give it all a stir, making sure the grains of rice are submerged. Replace the lid on the pot and cook on high for a further 45 minutes.

When ready to serve, top the rice bake with the grated cheese and sliced jalapeños, then cook with the lid off for a final 10 minutes or until the cheese has melted.

Divide the rice bake between deep bowls, then top with the crushed tortilla chips and any of your favourite toppings, including salsa, guacamole and soured cream.

COOK'S TIP

If you know you're going to have some leftover rice bake, add the crushed tortilla chips to each separate portion once it's plated up. If you add them and then reheat the rice bake, the tortilla chips will go soggy.

CHICKEN TIKKA RICE BAKE

SERVES 4

This all-in-one, slow-cooked dish means you can enjoy all the tastes of a succulent chicken tikka without the faff of having to boil rice separately to serve with the curry. I love this tikka rice bake with an extra dollop of plain yoghurt and a bit of hot sauce or mango chutney on the side.

- Cooking time: 1 hour on high; 2 hours on low
- Preparation time: 5 minutes
- Calories: 488 kcals per serving

70g tikka masala spice paste

50g natural yoghurt

500g boneless, skinless chicken thighs, cut into finger-width strips

220g basmati rice, soaked in boiling water for 5 minutes, then drained and rinsed

1 onion, roughly chopped

1 pepper (any colour), roughly chopped

1 tablespoon tomato purée

1 teaspoon ground cumin

1 teaspoon ground coriander

300ml passata

Juice of 1 lemon

10g coriander, chopped

Combine the tikka masala paste and yoghurt in a shallow bowl. Add the chicken to the bowl, then stir to make sure all the pieces are evenly coated in the spicy yoghurt. Set aside to marinate for at least 30 minutes but preferably for 2–3 hours if you have the time.

Put the rice, onion, pepper, tomato purée, ground cumin and ground coriander in the pot of the slow cooker. Pour in the passata, along with 100ml water, making sure all the grains of rice are submerged. Season with plenty of salt and pepper, then top with the marinated chicken. Cover the pot with the lid.

Set the slow cooker to 'cook' mode, then turn it either to high and cook for 1 hour or to low and cook for 2 hours.

When ready to serve, stir through the lemon juice and scatter in most of the chopped coriander, mixing the chicken through the rice.

Spoon the rice bake into shallow bowls or deep plates, then finish with the remaining chopped coriander.

COOK'S TIP

If you have the time, leave the chicken to marinate in the fridge for a few hours or even overnight. The longer the chicken is left to marinate, the more flavourful it will be.

HARISSA COD WITH CHORIZO AND BUTTER BEANS

SERVES 4

Butter beans are available in handy tins and are a really great store cupboard ingredient. However, for this recipe where the beans are front and centre, it's worth spending a little more on a jar of butter beans as they tend to be better quality. The beans make this a really hearty dish, without being heavy. Without the cod, the butter beans and chorizo are an exceptionally tasty duo.

Cooking time: 2 hours 5 minutes on low

Preparation time: 10 minutes

Calories: 403 kcals per serving (without bread)

120g chorizo, diced

2 garlic cloves, crushed

3 tablespoons harissa paste

1 tablespoon tomato purée

1 x 400g tin or jar butter beans (drained weight)

400ml passata

4 cod fillets (about 560g)

Salt and freshly ground black pepper

Optional – If it has one, set the slow cooker to 'fry' mode (or use a frying pan on the hob for this stage). Put the chorizo in the pot of the slow cooker or frying pan and cook for 3–4 minutes, or until the chorizo starts to release its oil. (You can skip this stage, but searing the chorizo does help to release its oil and lock in the flavour.)

Add the garlic, harissa paste and tomato purée to the pot of the slow cooker along with the chorizo. Tip in the butter beans and passata, then stir to mix well. Nestle the cod fillets in amongst the beans and chorizo, then season well with salt and pepper. Cover the pot with the lid.

Set the slow cooker to 'cook' mode, then turn it to low and cook for 2 hours.

When ready to serve, spoon the beans and chorizo into shallow bowls or deep plates and serve with hunks of crusty bread for mopping up the juices!

CREAMY SALMON WITH POTATOES

SERVES 4

If you're in the mood for a filling meal that's light in calories but loaded with flavour, this is a healthy one-pan dish. The creamy sauce goes so well with the salmon, broccoli and potatoes, while the capers added at the end have a salty kick that cuts through the richness.

- Cooking time: 1 hour 5 minutes on high; 2 hours 5 minutes on low
- Preparation time: 5 minutes
- Calories: 514 kcals per serving

750g baby potatoes, halved or quartered to roughly 2cm cubes

1 small head broccoli (about 300g), cut into florets the same size as the potatoes

230ml hot vegetable stock

4 salmon pieces (about 480g)

120g light cream cheese

1 tablespoon wholegrain mustard

½ tablespoon cornflour

30g Parmesan, grated

2 tablespoons drained capers (optional)

Salt and freshly ground black pepper

Put the potatoes and broccoli in the pot of the slow cooker, covering the base. Pour over the stock, then top with the salmon pieces. Season well with salt and pepper. Cover the pot with the lid.

Set the slow cooker to 'cook' mode, then turn it either to high and cook for 1 hour or to low and cook for 2 hours.

Carefully remove the salmon and broccoli from the slow cooker and transfer to plates.

Add the cream cheese, mustard, cornflour and Parmesan to the pot of the slow cooker with the potatoes, then season with a good grinding of black pepper. Stir well and cook on high, with the lid off, for a further 5 minutes or until thickened.

Lift the potatoes onto the plates alongside the salmon and broccoli, then spoon over the creamy sauce and scatter over the capers (if using).

TUNA PASTA BAKE

SERVES 4

This is one for the tuna lovers! My ultimate tuna pasta bake, except done in the slow cooker. The cherry tomatoes give it a sweetness. The mozzarella gives it a creaminess. All you need to do is give the dish time so that all the flavours can mix together.

🍲 Cooking time: 1 hour 40 minutes on high; 3 hours 20 minutes on low

🥘 Preparation time: 5 minutes

♡ Calories: 440 kcals per serving

2 x 145g tins tuna (in brine), drained

400g cherry tomatoes, halved

200g fusilli or conchiglie (or any other spiral- or shell-shaped pasta)

100g cream cheese

1 tablespoon tomato purée

300ml boiling water

1 x 125g ball mozzarella, torn

40g Cheddar, grated

Salt and freshly ground black pepper

Put the tuna, cherry tomatoes and pasta in the pot of the slow cooker, covering the base.

In a jug, combine the cream cheese, tomato purée and boiling water. Pour this cream cheese mixture over the tuna, tomatoes and pasta in the pot, then stir to mix everything together. Season well with plenty of salt and pepper. Cover the pot with the lid.

Set the slow cooker to 'cook' mode, then turn it either to high and cook for 1 hour or to low and cook for 2 hours.

Next, stir the torn mozzarella through the tuna pasta and scatter the grated Cheddar over the top. Replace the lid, then cook on high for a further 40 minutes or on low for a further 1 hour 20 minutes.

COOK'S TIP

If you need to leave this pasta bake in the slow cooker for longer, stir through the mozzarella at the start and cook for the full cooking time, then top with the Cheddar for the final 10 minutes.

PESTO AND PEA PASTA

Everyone's favourite easy pasta meal is made even more stress-free in the slow cooker. Sometimes shop-bought green pesto can have a bit of a harsh twang to it, but adding soft cream cheese and grated Parmesan takes the edge off the pesto to make a soft and smooth pasta dish.

 Cooking time: 1 hour on high; 2 hours on low

 Preparation time: 5 minutes

 Calories: 462 kcals per serving (based on 4 servings)

200g pasta (any shape you like)

1 x 160g jar or tub green pesto

350ml hot vegetable stock

150g frozen garden peas, defrosted in hot water

2 tablespoons cream cheese (I use Philadelphia)

40g Parmesan, grated

10g basil leaves, roughly chopped, plus extra to serve

Put the pasta in the pot of the slow cooker, in a single layer covering the base.

In a jug, combine the pesto and vegetable stock. Pour the pesto mixture over the pasta and stir to mix well. Cover the pot with the lid.

Set the slow cooker to 'cook' mode, then turn it to high and cook for 1 hour or turn it to low and cook for 2 hours.

Next, stir through the peas, cream cheese, Parmesan and basil, allowing the cream cheese to melt into the pasta.

Spoon the pasta pesto into deep bowls and top with a little extra basil.

CHICKEN FAJITA PASTA

Fajitas are a weeknight staple for so many of us, but I like to switch things up sometimes and serve it with pasta instead of the usual wraps. It makes more of a hearty meal, which I guarantee will become a family favourite! If you're really missing bread, then garlic bread always makes a delicious side.

- Cooking time: 1 hour 15 minutes on high; 2 hours 45 minutes on low
- Preparation time: 5 minutes
- Calories: 531 kcals per serving

2 large skinless chicken breasts (about 350g), diced

½ red onion, diced

1 pepper (any colour – I use red and yellow), diced

1 teaspoon garlic paste

2 tablespoons tomato purée

1 x 35g sachet fajita seasoning

1 teaspoon smoked paprika

300g fusilli (or any other spiral-shaped pasta)

600ml semi-skimmed milk

60g grated red Leicester and Cheddar mix

Salt and freshly ground black pepper

Put the chicken, onion, pepper, garlic paste and tomato purée in the pot of the slow cooker. Sprinkle over the fajita seasoning, smoked paprika and a pinch each of salt and pepper. Give everything a good stir, then cover the pot with the lid.

Set the slow cooker to 'cook' mode, then turn it either to high and cook for 30 minutes or to low and cook for 2 hours.

Next, add the pasta to the pot, then pour over the milk and stir well. Cook on high for a further 40 minutes, or until the pasta is cooked through.

When ready to serve, top the pasta with the grated cheese, put the lid back on the pot and cook until the cheese has melted. Stir once more before serving.

SPINACH AND RICOTTA PASTA SHELLS

SERVES 4

There's something so satisfying about filling these pasta shells that makes a slightly fiddly process feel incredibly rewarding! I've filled them with the classic ravioli-style filling for a veggie dish, but it's an easily adaptable recipe – you could even fill them with some leftover Bolognese Sauce (see page 108). I've made the grated Cheddar optional because it's quite a light dish without it, but some cheese is a nice add-on if you want an extra bit of comfort.

 Cooking time: 2 hours on low

 Preparation time: 20 minutes

♡ Calories: 275 kcals per serving (without cheese)

150g conchiglioni (or any shell-shaped pasta large enough to stuff)

200g baby spinach

250g ricotta

30g Parmesan, grated (vegetarian, if necessary)

Zest of 1 lemon

600ml passata with basil (or with garlic and herbs)

1 tablespoon tomato purée

1 teaspoon sugar

60g Cheddar, grated (optional)

Soak the pasta shells in boiling water for 10 minutes, then drain and leave to cool.

Put the spinach in a colander, place it in the sink and pour some just-boiled water over the spinach leaves until they wilt. Let them cool, drain in the colander (using a ladle to push it backwards into the colander), then roughly chop.

In a small bowl, mix the ricotta, Parmesan and lemon zest.

When they're cool enough to handle, spoon the ricotta mixture into the pasta shells, filling them as generously as possible (you could even pipe it in).

Pour the passata into the pot of the slow cooker, covering the base. Stir through the tomato purée and sugar. Lay the filled pasta shells in the passata, then cover the pot with the lid.

Set the slow cooker to 'cook' mode, then turn it to low and cook for 2 hours.

If using, 15 minutes before the end of the cooking time, scatter over the grated Cheddar and cook, with the lid on, until the cheese has melted.

CHAPTER 5

WEEKEND SPECIALS

BEEF AND MUSHROOMS IN PEPPERCORN SAUCE

SERVES 4-6

Beef with peppercorn sauce is a classic combo, but here I've added mushrooms too. In the slow cooker, the beef becomes really tender – it melts in the mouth in the creamy, mustardy sauce. I use two types of mustard for the sauce – the Dijon adds warmth and the wholegrain brings a fun texture as the seeds pop! You can use just one type of mustard, based on whatever you have in the cupboard.

 Cooking time: 4 hours 20 minutes on high; 8 hours 20 minutes on low

 Preparation time: 5 minutes

 Calories: 596 kcals per serving (based on 4 servings, without rice or mash)

½ tablespoon sunflower oil

400g chestnut mushrooms, sliced

2 onions, finely chopped

1kg extra-lean diced beef

1½ tablespoons flour

½ tablespoon peppercorns, crushed in a pestle and mortar

4 garlic cloves, crushed

1 teaspoon smoked paprika

3 tablespoons Dijon mustard

3 tablespoons wholegrain mustard

250ml hot beef stock

120ml soured cream

Salt and freshly ground black pepper

To serve

Rice or mashed potato

2 tablespoons crispy onions

If it has one, set the slow cooker to 'fry' mode (or use a frying pan on a hob for this stage). Add ½ tablespoon of the sunflower oil to the pot of the slow cooker or frying pan, followed by the mushrooms. Season the mushrooms with plenty of salt and pepper, then cook for 10–12 minutes. Transfer the mushrooms to a bowl, let them cool and then refrigerate until needed later.

Set the slow cooker to 'cook' mode, then turn it to high. Add the other ½ tablespoon of sunflower oil to the pot of the slow cooker, followed by the onions.

Season the beef, then toss the pieces in the flour. Add the beef to the pot with the onion and cook them together for 5 minutes.

Add the peppercorns, garlic, paprika and 1 tablespoon of each type of mustard to the pot. Pour the stock over the beef, then cover the pot with the lid.

With the slow cooker on 'cook' mode, either turn it to high and cook for 4 hours or turn it to low and cook for 8 hours.

Once the beef is cooked, return the mushrooms to the slow cooker along with the soured cream and remaining 2 tablespoons of each mustard. Season everything with plenty of black pepper.

Spoon the beef and mushrooms into deep bowls, on top of some rice or mash, if you like. Scatter over the crispy onions before serving.

LAZY LASAGNE

SERVES 6

We all adore a lasagne. The hearty meat sauce, the creamy béchamel, the cheesy, golden topping – what's not to love? The hassle of making it, that's what! This 'lazy' version gives you all the delicious flavours of lasagne, minus the fuss.

 Cooking time: 4 hours 50 minutes on high; 8 hours 50 minutes on low

 Preparation time: 15 minutes

Calories: 512 kcals per serving

500g beef mince (5% fat)

1 beef stock pot

Non-stick spray oil

1 onion, diced

80g carrots, grated

2 celery stalks, diced

1 pepper (any colour), diced

1 teaspoon garlic paste

2 tablespoons tomato purée

1 teaspoon dried oregano

1 teaspoon dried basil

1 teaspoon chilli flakes

1 teaspoon sugar

1 x 187ml bottle red wine (I use merlot)

1 tablespoon balsamic vinegar

1 x 500ml carton passata

1 x 40g packet Cheddar cheese sauce mix

300ml semi-skimmed milk

400g dried lasagne sheets

60g mozzarella, grated

Handful of chopped parsley, to serve

Salt and freshly ground black pepper

Optional – If it has one, set the slow cooker to 'fry' mode (or use a frying pan on the hob for this stage). Add the beef mince to the pot of the slow cooker or frying pan along with the stock pot, spritz with a few pumps of spray oil and cook for 7–8 minutes or until lightly browned. (You can skip this stage, but browning the mince helps lock in the flavour.)

Put the onion, carrots, celery and pepper into the pot of the slow cooker along with the mince and stock pot.

Add the garlic paste, tomato purée, oregano, basil, chilli flakes, sugar, red wine and vinegar to the pot, then season with a pinch each of salt and pepper.

Pour in the passata. Fill the empty passata carton with water, swirl it around and add that to the pot and give everything a good stir. Cover the pot with the lid.

Set the slow cooker to 'cook' mode, then turn it either to high and cook for 4 hours or to low and cook for 8 hours.

In a jug, combine the cheese sauce mix with the milk, whisking until smooth. Pour half of this cheese sauce into the lasagne mixture. Break the dried lasagne sheets into shards and stir those into the pot. Cook on high, with the lid on, for a further 40 minutes or until the pasta is cooked.

Pour the remaining cheese sauce over the top of the lasagne, then scatter with the grated mozzarella. Replace the lid on the pot, then leave the cheese to melt.

Sprinkle over the chopped parsley before serving.

COOK'S TIP

Make sure you mix the broken-up lasagne sheets into the lasagne mixture really well to avoid pieces of pasta sticking together.

HAM, MUSHROOM AND PEA RISOTTO

SERVES 6

Imagine if you could make a gorgeously creamy risotto without having to constantly stir the rice? Well, actually you can. The slow cooker is here to make all your fuss-free risotto dreams come true. Once the leeks, garlic and mushrooms have been sautéed and the rice has been toasted, the stock then goes in and from that point onwards it is entirely hands off.

 Cooking time: 1 hour 15 minutes on high; 2 hours 15 minutes on low

 Preparation time: 10 minutes

♡ Calories: 346 kcals per serving

1 tablespoon olive oil

300g chestnut mushrooms, thinly sliced

2 leeks, thinly sliced

2 garlic cloves, thinly sliced

350g risotto rice (I use arborio)

150ml white wine

800ml hot chicken stock

2 tablespoons cream cheese

2 tablespoons boiling water

150g sliced ham, chopped

150g frozen garden peas, defrosted in hot water

40g Parmesan, grated, plus extra to serve

Freshly ground black pepper

If it has one, set the slow cooker to 'fry' mode (or use a frying pan on the hob for this stage). Add the olive oil to the pot of the slow cooker or frying pan and allow it to heat up. Add the mushrooms, leeks and garlic and cook for 6 minutes or until softened.

Set the slow cooker to 'cook' mode, then turn it to high. Put the risotto rice in the pot of the slow cooker and cook on high for 1 minute. Pour in the white wine and cook for a further 2–3 minutes, or until the wine has mostly evaporated.

Add the stock to the pot and stir to combine, making sure all the grains of rice are fully submerged. Cover the pot with the lid.

Switch the slow cooker either to high and cook for 1 hour or to low and cook for 2 hours.

In a jug, combine the cream cheese with the boiling water. Stir this cream cheese mixture into the risotto along with the ham, peas and Parmesan. Season the risotto with a good grinding of black pepper.

When ready to serve, spoon the risotto into bowls and top with a little extra grated Parmesan.

COOK'S TIP

If you've made my Cola-Glazed Ham on page 175 and are looking for ways to use up any leftovers, stir them into this risotto.

GREEK-STYLE LAMB SHANKS IN WHITE WINE SAUCE

**SERVES
4**

The aroma of the fresh herbs in this dish is amazing – it makes you feel as though you're on a warm Greek island. I love these lamb shanks with mash, which mingles beautifully with the white wine sauce, but some baby potatoes are brilliant here too.

Cooking time: 8 hours 5 minutes on low

Preparation time: 10 minutes

Calories: 557 kcals per serving (without mash)

4 x small lamb shanks (about 400g)

1 onion, sliced

1 garlic bulb, halved

2 lemons, quartered

3 fresh rosemary sprigs

10g fresh oregano sprigs

375ml white wine

500ml hot chicken stock

1 tablespoon cornflour

10g fresh parsley, chopped

Salt and freshly ground black pepper

Place the lamb shanks in the pot of the slow cooker, laying them flat on the base.

Tuck the onion, garlic, lemons, rosemary and oregano around the lamb, then season well with salt and pepper.

Pour the white wine and chicken stock over the lamb shanks. Cover the pot with the lid.

Set the slow cooker to 'cook' mode, then turn it to low and cook for 8 hours.

Carefully remove the lamb shanks to a platter. Strain the white wine sauce from the pot into a saucepan, removing as much of the fat as possible.

Combine 2 tablespoons of the sauce with the cornflour in a small bowl, then mix to a smooth paste. Whisk this paste back into the sauce and put the saucepan over a medium-high heat. Continue to whisk for 2–3 minutes, or until the sauce has thickened.

Pour half the sauce over the lamb shanks and transfer the other half into a gravy jug.

Dot the lamb shanks with some of the slow-cooked onions from the pot and scatter over the chopped parsley.

COOK'S TIP

You can make this an all-in-one meal by adding small waxy potatoes (like new potatoes) to the pot of the slow cooker and cooking them alongside the lamb shanks and onion.

CHORIZO AND PRAWN JAMBALAYA

SERVES 4-6

Cajun seasoning is a genius cheat ingredient as it gives a dish all the flavours of the Deep South in a handy spice blend. The rice absorbs all these spices, as well as the smokiness of the chorizo from its delicious oil. Soaking the rice doesn't take long and it is important as it kicks off the cooking process and makes sure the rice doesn't have too much bite.

 Cooking time: 1 hour 25 minutes on high; 2 hours 40 minutes on low

 Preparation time: 5 minutes

 Calories: 449 kcals per serving (based on 4 servings)

120g chorizo, diced

1 onion, chopped

2 celery stalks, chopped

1 red pepper, diced

220g long-grain rice, soaked in boiling water for 5 minutes, then drained

1 heaped tablespoon Cajun seasoning

1 x 400g tin chopped tomatoes

100ml boiling water

330g raw king prawns

If it has one, set the slow cooker to 'fry' mode (or use a frying pan on the hob for this stage). Put the chorizo in the pot of the slow cooker or frying pan and cook for 2–3 minutes, or until the chorizo releases its oil.

Set the slow cooker to 'cook' mode, then turn it to high. Put the onion, celery and red pepper in the pot of the slow cooker along with the chorizo and cook for 2–3 minutes.

Next, add the drained rice to the pot along with the Cajun seasoning. Turn the rice in the chorizo oil.

Pour the chopped tomatoes and boiling water into the pot, then cover the pot with the lid.

Still on 'cook' mode, switch the slow cooker either to high and cook for 1 hour or to low and cook for 2 hours.

Gently stir the rice with a fork, then add the prawns, put the lid back on and cook for a further 12–15 minutes on high or 20–30 minutes on low, or until the prawns are pink and cooked through.

COOK'S TIP

Rather than using prawns, you could add diced chicken breasts to this jambalaya-style dish instead. Add it at the beginning of the cooking process, alongside the chorizo.

JERK-STYLE CHICKEN RICE BOWL

SERVES 4

Now that jerk spice paste is available in supermarkets, it's super easy to enjoy this Caribbean-style rice dish. For less heat, you can skip the scotch bonnet chilli. You could also use grilled corn cobs rather than sweetcorn kernels from a tin.

- Cooking time: 1 hour 30 minutes on high; 3 hours on low
- Preparation time: 5 minutes
- Calories: 534 kcals per serving

4 boneless, skinless chicken thighs, cut into finger-width strips

1–2 tablespoons jerk spice paste (I use Dunn's River)

220g long-grain rice, rinsed and drained

1 x 400g tin kidney beans, drained and rinsed

3 spring onions, chopped

1 scotch bonnet chilli (optional)

½ teaspoon allspice

1 x 400ml tin light coconut milk

1 x 325g tin sweetcorn kernels, drained

Jerk barbecue sauce, to serve

Put the chicken in a shallow bowl, spoon over the jerk paste and mix to combine, making sure the chicken is evenly coated.

Put the chicken in the pot of the slow cooker, covering the base. Top the chicken with the drained rice, kidney beans and spring onions. Add the scotch bonnet chilli (if using) and sprinkle over the allspice. Pour the coconut milk into the pot, making sure all the grains of rice are fully submerged. Cover the pot with the lid.

Set the slow cooker to 'cook' mode, then turn it either to high and cook for 1 hour 30 minutes or to low and cook for 3 hours.

When ready to serve, remove the scotch bonnet (if used) and stir the sweetcorn kernels through the rice. Serve with some jerk barbecue sauce, if you like.

CHEESY RANCH CHICKEN

SERVES 4

This chicken dinner is so tasty that it's dangerously addictive – one bite will never be enough! In case you've never come across it before, ranch dressing is a creamy buttermilk dressing with lots of garlic and herbs that is super popular in America. I've used it here to make a chicken dish that ticks all the boxes – creamy, crunchy, salty, cheesy. My recipe serves four, but only if everyone grabs their portion quickly.

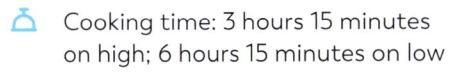 Cooking time: 3 hours 15 minutes on high; 6 hours 15 minutes on low

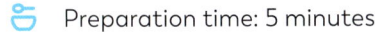 Preparation time: 5 minutes

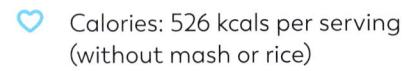 Calories: 526 kcals per serving (without mash or rice)

6 boneless, skinless chicken thighs (about 640g)

150ml ranch dressing

150g light cream cheese (I use Philadelphia)

1 teaspoon garlic granules

1 teaspoon onion granules

1 teaspoon cornflour

50g crispy smoked bacon rashers, chopped into small pieces

100g Cheddar cheese, grated

2 spring onions, thinly sliced

Put the chicken thighs into the pot of the slow cooker, covering the base.

Cover the chicken with the ranch dressing, dot with the cream cheese, then scatter over the garlic granules and onion granules. Cover the pot with the lid.

Set the slow cooker to 'cook' mode, then turn it either to high and cook for 3 hours or to low and cook for 6 hours.

Once cooked, transfer the chicken to a board and shred with two forks.

Remove 2 tablespoons of the creamy sauce from the pot and combine with the cornflour in a small bowl to make a smooth paste. Return this cornflour paste to the pot.

Return the shredded chicken to the pot and toss through the creamy sauce. Top with the bacon bits and grated Cheddar, then cook on high for a further 15 minutes or until the cheese has melted.

When ready to serve, scatter over the sliced spring onions and serve the chicken with mashed potato or steamed rice.

CHICKEN AND CHORIZO JACKET POTATOES

SERVES 4

A simple, slow-cooked jacket potato shows the joy of this magic gadget! Pop the spuds on first thing in the morning and they'll be ready for lunch. If you've batch cooked the chicken and chorizo, all you need to do is warm it up before loading it into the potatoes.

⏲ Cooking time for the jacket potatoes: 5 hours on high; 8 hours on low. Cooking time for the bake: 2 hours 35 minutes on high; 4 hours 35 minutes on low

🍲 Preparation time: 10 minutes

♡ Calories: 450 kcals per serving (with jacket potato)

For the chicken and chorizo bake

100g chorizo, sliced into thick coins

1 red onion, chopped

2 garlic cloves, crushed

1 teaspoon sweet smoked paprika

100g sundried tomatoes, drained and roughly chopped

2 x 400g tins chopped tomatoes

1 tablespoon red wine vinegar

1 teaspoon sugar

500g skinless chicken breasts, cut into bite-sized pieces

For the jacket potatoes

4 medium baking potatoes (about 180g each)

2 tablespoons sunflower oil

Salt and freshly ground black pepper

To prepare the jackets, rub the potatoes with the oil and season well with plenty of salt and pepper. Wrap each one individually in foil and stack in the pot of the slow cooker. Cover the pot with the lid.

Set the slow cooker to 'cook' mode, then turn it either to high and cook for 5 hours or to low and cook for 8 hours.

To prepare the chicken and chorizo, set the slow cooker to 'fry' mode (or use a frying pan on a hob for this stage). Put the chorizo in the pot of the slow cooker or frying pan and cook for 3–4 minutes, or until the chorizo releases its oil.

Add the onion, garlic, paprika and sundried tomatoes to the pot, stirring to coat everything in the chorizo oil.

Next, stir in the chopped tomatoes, vinegar and sugar, followed by the chicken. Season well with plenty of salt and pepper, then cover the pot with the lid.

Switch the slow cooker either to high and cook for 2 hours or to low and cook for 4 hours.

Remove the lid from the pot and cook on high for a further 30 minutes or until the sauce has thickened.

COOK'S TIP

Jacket potatoes are perfect for loading with baked beans, tuna or bacon bits or using up the last portion of beef chilli (see page 76). I like to mash the fluffy inside of a potato with some cream cheese and stir through a few chopped chives or spring onions. Spoon that mixture back into the skins, top with grated Cheddar and melt the cheese in the slow cooker.

MOROCCAN-STYLE CHICKEN STEW

SERVES 4-6

Chicken thighs in the slow cooker just have so much flavour, plus they stay nice and juicy. Here they're part of a lightly spiced stew, which is warming but not hot. You might have noticed that some chopped lemons go into the pot, with their skins and everything – if you like, you can eat the lemon skin as it cooks beautifully and develops a kind of caramelised taste!

 Cooking time: 3 hours 10 minutes on high; 6 hours 10 minutes on low

 Preparation time: 10 minutes

 Calories: 270 kcals per serving (based on 6 servings, without couscous or rice)

For the stew

2 red onions, sliced

1 tablespoon sunflower oil

3 garlic cloves, sliced

6 boneless, skinless chicken thighs (about 640g), chopped in half

1 tablespoon ground cinnamon

1 tablespoon ground cumin

½ tablespoon ground ginger

1 teaspoon ground turmeric

2 lemons (skin left on), finely chopped and pips removed

300ml hot chicken stock

40g raisins

1 tablespoon honey

Salt and freshly ground black pepper

To serve (optional)

60g green olives, roughly chopped

10g toasted flaked almonds

5g coriander or parsley, roughly chopped

Optional – If it has one, set the slow cooker to 'fry' mode (or use a frying pan on the hob for this stage). Put the red onions in the pot of the slow cooker or frying pan with the sunflower oil and cook for 7 minutes, or until softened.

Put all the ingredients for the stew (except the raisins and honey) in the pot of the slow cooker along with the red onions. Season well with plenty of salt and pepper. Cover the pot with the lid.

Set the slow cooker to 'cook' mode, then turn it to high and cook for 2 hours 30 minutes or to low and cook for 5 hours 30 minutes.

Stir the raisins and honey into the stew, replace the lid and continue to cook for a further 30 minutes.

When ready to serve, scatter over the chopped olives and flaked almonds, then finish with a handful of chopped coriander or parsley.

MARRY ME CHICKEN

SERVES 4

This recipe is so delicious that it might just get someone so loved up that they propose! There are lots of variations on this recipe – some with sundried tomatoes, some without – but mine is made with a mushroom and wine sauce. To me, this is perfection. It's a really versatile dish, which you can serve with pasta, rice or potatoes.

 Cooking time: 3 hours 25 minutes on high; 6 hours 25 minutes on low

 Preparation time: 5 minutes

♡ Calories: 357 kcals per serving

4 chicken breasts (about 600g)

1 teaspoon Italian-style seasoning, plus an extra pinch

1 teaspoon dried chilli flakes, plus an extra pinch

1 tablespoon plain flour

1 tablespoon olive oil

1 onion, sliced

200g baby button or chestnut mushrooms, halved

1 teaspoon garlic paste

1 chicken stock pot

125ml Prosecco (or white wine)

100ml double cream (I use Elmlea)

30g Parmesan, grated

2 teaspoons cornflour

Salt and freshly ground black pepper

To serve

300g tagliatelle (or any other thick ribbon-shaped pasta), cooked to the packet instructions

Pinch of dried chilli flakes

Season the chicken breasts with the Italian-style seasoning, chilli flakes and plenty of salt and pepper, then dust the chicken in the flour.

If it has one, set the slow cooker to 'fry' mode (or use a frying pan on the hob for this stage). Put the olive oil in the pot of the slow cook or frying pan, then once it is warm add the chicken and cook for 7–8 minutes or until lightly browned on both sides. Transfer the chicken to a plate and set aside.

Next, add the onion and mushrooms to the same oil in either the slow cooker pot or pan, then cook for 5–6 minutes to soften.

Combine the sautéed chicken, onions and mushrooms in the pot of the slow cooker, then add the garlic paste, stock pot, another pinch each of the Italian-style seasoning and chilli flakes. Pour the Prosecco into the pot, then cover with the lid.

Set the slow cooker to 'cook' mode, then either turn it to high and cook for 3 hours or turn it to low and cook for 6 hours.

Once the chicken is cooked through, stir in the cream and Parmesan.

Remove 2 tablespoons of the liquid from the pot and put it in a small bowl. Add the cornflour and mix to a smooth paste. Return the cornflour paste to the slow cooker and mix to combine, then cook with the lid off for a further 8–10 minutes to thicken.

When ready, serve the marry me chicken over cooked tagliatelle and with an extra pinch of chilli flakes.

CREAMY SUNDRIED TOMATO AND SPINACH GNOCCHI

**SERVES
4**

Sundried tomatoes are such a great 'cheat' ingredient – they add so much flavour for absolutely no effort! This meal feels light and fresh thanks to the summery vegetables and herbs, but has that comforting feel due to the creamy sauce and fluffy gnocchi.

 Cooking time: 1 hour 45 minutes on low

 Preparation time: 5 minutes

 Calories: 413 kcals per serving

280g light cream cheese (I use Philadelphia)

2 garlic cloves, crushed

1 x 280g jar sundried tomatoes, drained and chopped

250ml boiling water

200g baby spinach

500g potato gnocchi

30g Parmesan, grated, plus extra to serve

5g basil, leaves torn, plus extra to serve

Combine the cream cheese, garlic and sundried tomatoes in the pot of the slow cooker. Pour in 200ml of the boiling water and stir to mix everything together. Cover the pot with the lid.

Set the slow cooker to 'cook' mode, then turn it either to high and cook for 45 minutes or to low and cook for 1 hour 30 minutes.

Fold in the spinach with another 50ml boiling water, followed by the gnocchi and Parmesan, then cook on high for a final 15 minutes.

When ready, stir through the torn basil leaves and serve the gnocchi with a few extra basil leaves and a final sprinkle of Parmesan.

ORZO RAGÙ

SERVES 4

Ragù is often served with a ribbon-shaped pasta, such tagliatelle or pappardelle, but since I tried it with orzo, I haven't looked back. A tiny pasta shaped like grains of rice, orzo is great for soaking up lots of flavour from the sauce, so it marries perfectly with the rich ragù.

- Cooking time: 4 hours 55 minutes on high; 8 hours 55 minutes on low
- Preparation time: 10 minutes
- Calories: 549 kcals per serving

300g beef mince (5% fat)

1 red onion, diced

1 carrot, diced

100g button or chestnut mushrooms, finely chopped

1 red pepper, deseeded and diced

1 beef stock pot

1 teaspoon garlic paste

2 tablespoons tomato purée

1 teaspoon dried oregano

¼ teaspoon chilli flakes

1 x 400g tin chopped tomatoes

350g orzo

75g frozen garden peas

60ml double cream (I use Elmlea)

Handful of cherry tomatoes

30g Parmesan, grated

Salt and freshly ground black pepper

Optional – If it has one, set the slow cooker to 'fry' mode (or use a frying pan on a hob for this stage). Add the beef mince to the pot of the slow cooker or frying pan and cook for 7–8 minutes or until lightly browned. (You can skip this stage, but searing the beef mince does help to lock in the flavour.)

Put the onion, carrot, mushrooms and red pepper in the pot of the slow cooker along with the beef mince.

Next, add the stock pot, garlic paste, tomato purée, oregano, chilli flakes and a pinch each of salt and pepper.

Pour in the chopped tomatoes. Fill the empty tin with water, swirl it around and add that to the pot and give everything a good stir. Cover the pot with the lid.

Set the slow cooker to 'cook' mode, then turn it either to high and cook for 4 hours or to low and cook for 8 hours.

Add the orzo, frozen peas and cream, give everything a good stir, then cook on high for 45 minutes or until the orzo is cooked. If needed, add an extra splash of water to loosen things.

Once cooked, stir through the cherry tomatoes and Parmesan, then leave for 2–3 minutes or until everything is warmed through.

SHRIMP BOIL

I kept seeing seafood boils online, so I had to give it a go. By cooking them in beer, the prawns stay really moist and the potatoes just melt in the mouth as they soak up all the juices. Tail-on prawns are that much easier to eat with your hands, plus they look impressive as part of the platter.

 Cooking time: 2 hours on high

 Preparation time: 15 minutes

Calories: 539 kcals per serving (without bread)

1 onion, cut into wedges

2 large garlic cloves, sliced

500g red potatoes, cut into large chunks

4 mini corn on the cobs

300ml beer

200ml hot chicken or vegetable stock

4 spicy chorizo cooking sausages, thickly sliced (about 200g)

20 raw king prawns (tail-on, if possible)

Crusty baguette, to serve

For the garlic butter

100g unsalted butter

2 tablespoons garlic paste

1 tablespoon Old Bay or Cajun seasoning

2 teaspoons salt

Small bunch of parsley, finely chopped

Set the slow cooker to 'cook' mode, then turn it to high and leave to warm up.

Put the onion, garlic, potatoes and corn cobs in the pot of the slow cooker. Pour in the beer and stock, then cover the pot with the lid.

Cook on high for 1 hour 30 minutes.

Add the sausages and prawns to the pot and cook for a further 30 minutes or until the prawns have turned pink.

Meanwhile, prepare the garlic butter. Melt the butter in a pan (or alternatively use a microwave for this stage). Once foaming, add the garlic paste, seasoning and salt to the butter and cook for 1 minute. Stir through the parsley.

Line a large tray with parchment paper. Using a slotted spoon, carefully lift everything (except the onions) out of the slow cooker, let drain for a moment then transfer to the lined tray – you want as little of the cooking liquid as possible.

Drizzle the garlic butter over all the ingredients on the tray, then place on the table with hunks of crusty bread for mopping up the buttery juices.

COOK'S TIP

Feel free to use frozen jumbo prawns as they are a little more affordable.

CHILLI PRAWN AND PROSECCO LINGUINE

SERVES 4

If you're looking for an elegant but easy recipe for when you have guests coming over, then you're in the right place. The Prosecco lends a subtle flavour, but if you prefer things alcohol-free you can always use fish stock or just water instead. The chilli brings a little warmth to things, but if everyone likes more of a kick then leave the seeds in.

Cooking time: 1 hour 10 minutes on high; 2 hours 15 minutes on low

Preparation time: 5 minutes

Calories: 511 kcals per serving

275g linguine (or any other thin ribbon-shaped pasta), rinsed under boiling water

500g cherry tomatoes, halved

2 garlic cloves, crushed

1 red chilli, deseeded and chopped

1 x 375ml bottle Prosecco

90ml double cream (I use Elmlea)

Juice of 1 lemon

330g raw king prawns

5g parsley, chopped

Salt and freshly ground black pepper

Lay the linguine on the base of the slow cooker pot. Top with the tomatoes, garlic and chilli. Season well with plenty of salt and pepper, then pour over the Prosecco. Cover the pot with the lid.

Set the slow cooker to 'cook' mode, then turn it either to high and cook for 1 hour or to low and cook for 2 hours.

Next, stir through the double cream and lemon juice, along with 120ml water. Stir in the prawns, replace the lid and cook on high for a further 8–10 minutes or 15 minutes on low until the prawns are pink and cooked through.

If needed, add a splash more water to loosen up the pasta, then serve in bowls scattered with the chopped parsley.

CHAPTER
6

SUNDAY LUNCH

BEEF TOPSIDE

Searing the beef is optional, however caramelising the outer edges gives the meat maximum flavour and so it's worth spending a few minutes on. Then by sitting the beef over the veggies in the slow cooker, you create a really delicious gravy. To make sure your beef is cooked to your liking, I recommend using a digital thermometer as all joints vary in size. And because everyone loves Sunday roast leftovers, enjoy any remaining beef slices in sandwiches the next day.

Cooking time: 2 hours on high; 3 hours 30 minutes on low

Preparation time: 10 minutes

Calories: 405 kcals per serving

1.4kg beef topside roasting joint

1 onion, skin left on and cut into wedges

2 carrots, roughly chopped

2 celery stalks, roughly chopped

2 garlic cloves, skin left on and crushed

½ tablespoon sunflower oil

1 x 187ml bottle white wine

400ml hot beef stock

2 tablespoons tomato purée

2 rosemary sprigs

2 tablespoons cornflour

Salt and freshly ground black pepper

Season the beef joint well with plenty of salt and pepper.

Optional – Set the slow cooker to 'fry' mode (or use a frying pan on the hob for this stage). Put the beef joint in the pot of the slow cooker or frying pan and sear it on all sides until lightly browned. Transfer the beef to a plate and set aside.

Put the onion, carrots, celery and garlic in the pot of the slow cooker with the sunflower oil, then stir them around for 2–3 minutes to pick up some colour.

Add the wine to the pot with the veggies, followed by the stock, tomato purée and rosemary sprigs.

Place the wire rack insert in the slow cooker, so that it sits over the vegetables, and put the beef joint on the rack. Cover the pot with the lid.

Switch the slow cooker to 'cook' mode. For medium beef, cook on high for 1 hour 15 minutes–1 hour 30 minutes or low for 2 hours 30 minutes–3 hours.

Transfer the beef joint to a board and remove the wire rack insert from the pot. Using a slotted spoon, lift the vegetables out of the pot and place them in a serving dish.

While the beef rests, add 4 tablespoons of the gravy to the cornflour in a small bowl, then mix to a smooth paste. Stir the cornflour paste back into the gravy in the pot and cook on high for 15–20 minutes, or until the gravy has thickened.

When ready, slice the beef and serve with the veggies and gravy alongside.

COOK'S TIP

A meat thermometer is really helpful here as it's a great way to ensure your meat is cooked exactly to your liking. You want an internal temperature of 50°C for rare, 60°C for medium and 70°C for well-done.

COLA-GLAZED HAM

SERVES 6-8

This recipe transforms an uncooked gammon to a tasty cooked ham. By slow cooking the gammon in cola, all those signature spices of the fizzy drink permeate the meat. You can slice and serve the ham warm as soon as it comes out of the slow cooker, however, by popping it under a hot grill you end up with a sweet, succulent outer layer.

Cooking time: 4 hours on high; 8 hours on low

Preparation time: 10 minutes

Calories: 482 kcals per serving (cooked with zero-calorie cola and based on 8 servings)

For the gammon

2kg gammon

1 onion, cut into wedges

1 large carrot, roughly chopped

2 celery stalks, roughly chopped

2–2.5 litres zero-calorie cola (or you can use regular cola)

For the glaze

80g soft brown sugar

1 tablespoon chilli jam

2 tablespoons Dijon mustard

Put the gammon, onion, carrot and celery in the pot of the slow cooker. Pour over the cola, adding enough to make sure the gammon is covered. Cover the pot with the lid.

Set the slow cooker to 'cook' mode, then turn it to high and cook for 4 hours or turn it to low and cook for 7–8 hours, or until the meat is tender but not falling apart.

Carefully lift the cooked ham out of the slow cooker pot and transfer to a board. Allow the ham to rest and cool for 1 hour.

While the ham is cooling, prepare the glaze by combining the sugar, chilli jam and Dijon mustard in a bowl.

Once the ham is cool enough to handle, remove the outer layer of skin, but leaving the fat. Using a sharp knife, score lines into the layer of fat. Place the ham on a heatproof tray and spoon the glaze over the outer fat layer.

Place the ham under a preheated grill until the glaze on the fat layer is golden and bubbling. Slice before serving.

COOK'S TIP

I use zero-calorie cola for cooking the gammon, but as most of the liquid is discarded anyway, if you use regular cola then the difference in calories is minimal.

ROAST CHICKEN

This succulent herby 'roast' chicken takes all of the usual worries away from cooking your Sunday dinner – no more dry or undercooked chicken! I always like to stuff a lemon into mine to keep it extra juicy, and get a lovely layer of citrusy flavour in there to complement the herbs. Best served with crispy roast potatoes, your favourite veg and some stuffing, of course!

 Cooking time: 4–5 hours on high; 7–8 hours on low

 Preparation time: 10 minutes

♡ Calories: depends on the weight of the chicken (see label for details)

1 whole chicken (about 1.75–2kg, depending on the size of your slow cooker)

1 lemon, quartered

1 bay leaf

1 white onion, peeled and quartered

1 red onion, peeled and quartered

2 large carrots, chopped into large pieces (no need to peel)

Olive oil spray

2 teaspoons paprika

1 teaspoon garlic granules

1 teaspoon onion granules (or 1 teaspoon garlic paste)

1 teaspoon dried thyme

200ml hot chicken stock

Salt and freshly ground black pepper

Stuff the chicken with the lemon, bay leaf and a couple of the onion quarters. Arrange the remaining vegetables across the pot of the slow cooker to create a base for the chicken to sit on.

Spray the chicken skin with olive oil spray, then sprinkle over the paprika garlic granules, onion granules and dried thyme. Rub the seasonings into the skin so that the entire chicken is coated and season all over with salt and pepper.

Sit the chicken on top of the veggies in the pot of the slow cooker, then pour the stock into pot – the liquid should just reach the bottom of the chicken. Cover the pot with the lid.

Set the slow cooker to 'cook' mode, then turn it either to high and cook for 4–5 hours or to low for 7–8 hours.

Carefully lift the chicken out of the pot and transfer to a board. Leave the chicken to stand for 30 minutes before carving. You can cover the chicken with foil to keep it warm.

COOK'S TIP

For crispy chicken skin, pop the cooked chicken onto a roasting tray and place it under a preheated grill for 5–10 minutes before carving.

SHREDDED HOISIN DUCK

Duck makes a fun alternative to roast chicken for Sunday lunch, especially when it's served in Chinese-style pancakes. Cooking the duck in the slow cooker means the meat stays moist, plus resting it on the wire rack insert allows any fat to drain onto the base of the pot. It's then easy to wash up the pot, which makes it much cleaner than cooking in the oven, giving you time to enjoy your weekend.

 Cooking time: 5 hours on high; 10 hours on low

 Preparation time: 10 minutes

♡ Calories: 445 kcals per serving (based on 6 servings)

1 whole duck (about 1.75–2kg, depending on the size of your slow cooker), giblets removed

4 spring onions, halved

2 teaspoons Chinese five spice powder, plus an extra ¼ teaspoon

5 tablespoons hoisin sauce

To serve

20 Chinese pancakes, prepared to the packet instructions

Some extra hoisin sauce

4 spring onions, cut into three, then sliced thinly lengthways

½ cucumber, deseeded and cut into thin matchsticks

Pat the duck dry with kitchen paper, then fill the cavity with the halved spring onions.

Rub the skin of the duck with the Chinese five spice powder, sprinkling some into the cavity too.

Sit the duck on the wire rack insert in the pot of the slow cooker, then spoon 2 tablespoons of the hoisin sauce over the bird. Cover the pot with the lid.

Set the slow cooker to 'cook' mode, then turn it either to high and cook for 5 hours or to low for 10 hours.

Carefully lift the duck out of the pot and transfer to a board. Shred the meat with two forks, discarding the skin and bones.

Place the shredded duck meat in a bowl and mix in the remaining hoisin sauce and the extra ¼ teaspoon Chinese five spice powder.

Serve the hoisin duck with the warmed pancakes. Encourage everyone to spread a little extra hoisin sauce over the pancakes before topping with the hoisin duck, spring onions and cucumber sticks.

LEG OF LAMB COOKED IN RED WINE

SERVES 6

A leg of lamb is one of my favourite things to cook in the slow cooker. It's such an effortless, yet impressive dish to serve up to a crowd! Either buttery mash or Dauphinoise potatoes (see page 188) are a must with lamb, along with some greens. You could always serve the carrots that are added to the slow cooker. On the table, I always give my guests the options of mint sauce and redcurrant jelly.

 Cooking time: 8 hours on low

 Preparation time: 10 minutes

♡ Calories: 265 kcals per serving

1.2kg half leg of lamb

6 garlic cloves

Few rosemary sprigs

1 red onion, roughly chopped

2 carrots, roughly chopped

300ml red wine

300ml hot lamb stock (made with 1 lamb stock pot)

Salt and freshly ground black pepper

Make several small incisions in the lamb, then stuff each slit with a garlic clove and rosemary sprig.

Put the onion and carrots in the pot of the slow cooker. Rest the leg of lamb on top of the veggies, then season with salt and pepper.

Pour the wine and stock over the lamb, then cover the pot with the lid.

Set the slow cooker to 'cook' mode, then turn it to low and cook for 8 hours.

Once cooked, remove the garlic and rosemary from the slits in the lamb then take the lamb off the bone and slice or shred before serving.

COOK'S TIP

If you want to make a gravy, thicken the lamb juices left in the base of the slow cooker pot with 1–2 tablespoons of cornflour.

SMOKY FISH CHOWDER

SERVES 4

This is my take on a New England-style chowder. The smokiness from the haddock is amazing, which is enhanced by the bacon lardons. The lardons also bring a saltiness to balance out the sweetness of the corn kernels. You might think evaporated milk is only for desserts, but adding to this chunky soup makes it rich, moreish and special enough to serve up for Sunday lunch.

Cooking time: 1 hour 10 minutes on high; 2 hours 10 minutes on low

Preparation time: 10 minutes

Calories: 508 kcals per serving

80g smoked bacon lardons (optional)

1 carrot, peeled and diced

2 celery stalks, diced

600g smoked haddock (or salmon and hake), cut into rough 3cm chunks (or you can use 2 x 300g packs fish pie mix)

500g baby potatoes, halved (or quartered, if large)

300ml hot chicken or vegetable stock

2 teaspoons cornflour

250ml evaporated milk

1 x 325g tin sweetcorn kernels (260g drained weight)

Juice of 1 lemon

Salt and freshly ground black pepper

If it has one, set the slow cooker to 'fry' mode (or use a frying pan for this stage). If using, put the bacon lardons in the pot of the slow cooker or frying pan and cook for 2 minutes, or until lightly golden.

Add the carrot and celery to the pot with the bacon lardons and cook for a further 3–4 minutes or until they take on some colour.

Next, put the fish chunks and baby potatoes in the pot, then pour over the stock. Cover the pot with the lid.

Set the slow cooker to 'cook' mode, then turn it either to high and cook for 1 hour or to low and cook for 2 hours, or until the potatoes are soft.

Remove 2 tablespoons of the soup from the pot and add to a small bowl with the cornflour. Mix to a smooth paste then stir it back into the soup in the pot to thicken.

Lastly, stir in the evaporated milk and sweetcorn kernels. Check the seasoning and more salt and pepper, if needed, then adjust with some lemon juice to taste.

COOK'S TIP

Cutting the fish into chunks yourself will help it maintain its shape while it cooks, but using a prepared fish pie mix is a much quicker fix.

NUT ROAST

SERVES 6-8

Whether you're a meat eater or not, this nut roast makes a substantial meal and is a great option for Sunday lunch. Serve it with Yorkshire puddings and roasted veggies and then, if there's any leftover, enjoy it during the week with mash and onion gravy. It's a really flexible recipe – you can use up any half-empty packets of nuts or add in dried apricots in place of cranberries.

⏲ Cooking time: 3 hours 10 minutes on high; 6 hours 10 minutes on low

🥄 Preparation time: 10 minutes

♡ Calories: 512 kcals per serving (based on 6 servings)

2 tablespoons olive oil

1 onion, finely chopped

2 celery stalks, finely chopped

1 carrot, grated

3 thyme sprigs, leaves picked

300g mixed nuts, finely chopped

50g dried cranberries, roughly chopped

1 x 85g packet sage and onion stuffing

150ml boiling water

30g unsalted butter

1 egg, beaten

50g fresh breadcrumbs

Salt and freshly ground black pepper

Optional – If it has one, set the slow cooker to 'fry' mode (or use a frying pan on the hob for this stage). Heat the olive oil in the pot of the slow cooker or frying pan, then add the onion and celery and cook for 8–10 minutes, or until softened and translucent. (You can skip this stage, but frying the onion does help to kickstart the caramelisation process.)

In a mixing bowl, combine the onion, celery, carrot, thyme leaves, nuts and cranberries. Season well with plenty of salt and pepper.

Stir the stuffing mix into the boiling water, then mash in the butter. Add this stuffing to the mixing bowl with the nut and cranberry mixture.

Add the beaten egg and breadcrumbs to the mixing bowl along with the other two mixtures, then work everything together.

Oil a 2lb loaf tin or pudding basin, then line the base with parchment paper. Pack the nut roast into the loaf tin or pudding basin, then smooth over the top with the back of a spoon. Cover with a double layer of foil, tucking it tightly round the edges.

Place the wire rack insert or a trivet in the slow cooker pot, then sit the tin or basin on the rack or trivet. Cover the pot with the lid.

Set your slow cooker to 'cook' mode, then turn it either to high and cook for 3 hours or to low and cook for 6 hours.

Once cooked, let the nut roast sit for 30 minutes before turning it out on to a plate.

VEGGIE SAUSAGE CASSEROLE WITH MASHED POTATOES

SERVES 4

A bowl full of creamy mash topped with my favourite veggie sausages cooked in an onion gravy is a perfect Sunday lunch, especially when the weather is chilly. In the slow cooker, the fresh herbs infuse all the other ingredients and so the whole casserole tastes really aromatic. As an alternative to mash, sometimes I serve this sausage casserole in a giant Yorkshire pudding, which I make in my air fryer.

 Cooking time: 4 hours 15 minutes on high; 8 hours 15 minutes on low

 Preparation time: 15 minutes

 Calories: 572 kcals per serving (with mash)

For the casserole

8 veggie sausages

1 onion, diced

500g carrots, roughly chopped

2 leeks, sliced

1 tablespoon tomato purée

½ teaspoon rosemary leaves

½ teaspoon thyme leaves

1 bay leaf

500ml hot vegetable stock

3 tablespoons gravy granules

For the mash

1kg potatoes, peeled and cut into large chunks

Knob of butter

Salt and freshly ground black pepper

Optional – If it has one, set the slow cooker to 'fry' mode (or use a non-stick frying pan over a low–medium heat for this stage). Add the sausages to the dry pot of the slow cooker or pan and cook for 5 minutes or until lightly browned. (You can skip this stage, but searing the sausages helps to lock in the flavour.) Transfer the sausages to a bowl and set aside.

Put the onion, carrots, leeks, tomato purée and herbs in the pot of the slow cooker and cook on high for 10 minutes, or until softened.

Add the sausages to the pot and pour in the stock. Cover the pot with the lid.

Set the slow cooker to 'cook' mode, then turn it either to high and cook for 4 hours or to low and cook for 8 hours.

Once cooked, stir in the gravy granules to thicken the sauce. (You can add more or less granules, depending on how thick you like the sauce. Just remember, it will thicken up further when left overnight.)

With 15 minutes of the cooking time left, make the mash. Place the potatoes in a large pan of salted water. Bring to the boil over a high heat and cook the potatoes for about 15 minutes or until they're soft enough to mash. Once cooked, drain the potatoes, return them to the pan and roughly mash them. Add the knob of butter and continue to mash until smooth. Season the mash with salt and pepper to your taste.

When ready to serve, spoon some mash into individual bowls and then place the sausage casserole on top, making sure everyone gets two sausages each.

PERI-PERI MAC N CHEESE WITH BUTTERNUT SQUASH

SERVES 6-8

The peri-peri seasoning in this dish gives it a subtly spicy kick – a perfect contrast to the sweetness of the squash and the delicious cheesy sauce. This mac n cheese is a very welcome addition to the table for Sunday lunch, but it's also amazing as a meat-free meal on its own.

Cooking time: 1 hour 45 minutes on high; 3 hours 15 minutes on low

Preparation time: 10 minutes

Calories: 507 kcals per serving (based on 6 servings)

400g butternut squash, peeled and diced (about 1 small squash)

300g macaroni, rinsed under boiling water

200g mature Cheddar cheese, grated

2 tablespoons peri-peri seasoning (I use Nando's medium flavour shaker)

125g light cream cheese (I use Philadelphia)

700ml whole milk, plus an extra 200ml

100g grated mozzarella and Cheddar mix

Salt and freshly ground black pepper

Peri-peri sauce, to serve (optional)

Combine all the ingredients (except the extra 200ml milk and grated mozzarella and Cheddar mix) in the pot of the slow cooker. Mix everything together, then season with plenty of salt and pepper. Cover the pot with the lid.

Set the slow cooker to 'cook' mode, then turn it either to high and cook for 1 hour 30 minutes or to low and cook for 3 hours.

Stir through the remaining 200ml milk, if needed – you might not need this extra milk if the pasta hasn't absorbed all the liquid so far.

Top the mac n cheese with the grated mozzarella and Cheddar mix, then cook for a further 15 minutes on high, until melted.

Serve the mac n cheese with your choice of peri-peri sauce for drizzling over, if you like.

BROCCOLI AND CAULIFLOWER CHEESE

SERVES 4

For me, these cheese-smothered veggies complete any Sunday lunch. They're perfect as they are, but also go really well with some roast beef, chicken or ham. This is a super cheesy dish so try to use a lovely sharp and nutty mature Cheddar as the cheese is the star of the show.

 Cooking time: 2 hours 30 minutes on high; 5 hours on low

 Preparation time: 5 minutes

Calories: 545 kcals per serving

25g unsalted butter

50g flour

450ml whole milk

100g cream cheese

1 tablespoon wholegrain mustard

250g mature Cheddar, grated

1 medium head of broccoli, broken into florets (about 200g)

1 small-medium cauliflower (about 400g), broken into florets the same size as the broccoli

Salt and freshly ground black pepper

Set the slow cooker to 'cook' mode, then turn it to high. Put the butter, flour and milk in the pot of the slow cooker, then vigorously whisk everything together to make a smooth sauce with no lumps.

Stir the cream cheese, mustard and two-thirds of the grated Cheddar into the sauce in the pot. Season well with plenty of salt and pepper.

Fold the broccoli and cauliflower florets into the cheese sauce, making sure every piece is well coated. Top with the remaining grated Cheddar. Cover the pot with the lid.

Still on 'cook' mode, turn it either to high and cook for 2 hours 30 minutes or to low and cook for 5 hours.

COOK'S TIP

You can serve up this broccoli cauli cheese just as it is, or if you want to brown off the top then flash it under a hot grill to add a bit of colour. If the pot of your slow cooker lifts out and is heatproof, then you can pop the whole thing under the grill. If not, then ladle out the veggies and cheese sauce into an ovenproof tray.

DAUPHINOISE POTATOES

These potatoes are so incredibly moreish, I have to stop myself from eating them straight from the slow cooker pot. The Gruyère melts away to make the Dauphinoise extra creamy, without being too wet. Gruyère cheese has a delicious nuttiness but you can leave it out or swap it for Cheddar or Parmesan, if you're not a fan. Enjoy with your favourite main – or just as is!

Cooking time: 2 hours on high; 4 hours on low

Preparation time: 10 minutes

Calories: 321 kcals per serving

10g unsalted butter

800g potatoes, peeled and thinly sliced (I use King Edwards)

200ml double cream (I use Elmlea)

200ml chicken or vegetable stock

60g Gruyère cheese, grated

Salt and freshly ground black pepper

Rub the butter around the inside of the slow cooker pot.

Layer one-third of the sliced potatoes in the pot of the slow cooker, covering the base.

Mix the cream and stock in a jug, then pour roughly one-third of the cream mixture over the potatoes. Season well with plenty of salt and pepper, then scatter over some of the grated Gruyère.

Repeat the layers of potato slices, cream mixture and grated Gruyère twice more, until all the ingredients have been used up. Cover the pot with the lid.

Set the slow cooker to 'cook' mode, then turn it either to high and cook for 2 hours or to low and cook for 4 hours.

CHAPTER

7

DESSERTS & DRINKS

RICE PUDDING

SERVES 4

Rice pudding is such a comforting crowd-pleaser. Serve it warm out of the slow cooker, with your favourite jam or compote swirled through the rice, or try it cold straight from the fridge – both ways are delicious. Switch up the flavour with different jams; I love a blob of raspberry or strawberry jam.

Cooking time: 2 hours on high; 4 hours on low

Preparation time: none

Calories: 215 kcals per serving (without cream and jam)

15g unsalted butter

100g pudding rice

50g sugar

500ml whole milk (or use semi-skimmed milk, if that's what you have in the fridge)

To serve (optional)

Single cream

Your favourite fruit jam or compote

Rub the butter all over the inside of the slow cooker pot.

Put the rice and sugar in the pot, then pour over the milk along with 200ml water. Cover the pot with the lid.

Set the slow cooker to 'cook' mode, then turn it either to high and cook for 2 hours or to low and cook for 4 hours.

When ready to serve, ladle the rice pudding into bowls. Depending on how you like it, drizzle over some cream and top with a spoonful of fruit jam or compote.

COOK'S TIP

If you fancy cooking some fruit to go with this rice pudding, try my Stewed Strawberries (see page 195) or Cherry Bakewell Compote (see page 200).

STEWED STRAWBERRIES WITH SHORTBREAD AND CREAM

SERVES 4

This is summer in a bowl. It tastes exactly like a cream tea enjoyed on a sunny day, but with very little fuss. Serving the stewed strawberries slightly warm brings out their fruitiness, making them even more delicious. I serve some softly whipped cream and shortbread fingers with the strawberries, but you could try clotted cream and any crunchy biscuits you've got lying about the house.

- Cooking time: 2 hours 30 minutes on low
- Preparation time: 10 minutes, plus cooling
- Calories: 595 kcals per serving (with two shortbread fingers)

1kg strawberries, hulled and quartered

Juice of 1 lemon

200g sugar

2 tablespoons cornflour

To serve

100ml double cream

8 shortbread fingers

Put the strawberries in the pot of the slow cooker with the lemon juice and sugar. Cover the pot with the lid.

Set the slow cooker to 'cook' mode, then turn it to low and cook for 2 hours.

Remove 2 tablespoons of the strawberry juices from the slow cooker and mix with the cornflour in a small bowl to make a smooth paste. Stir the cornflour paste back into the pot and continue to cook, with the lid off, for a further 30 minutes.

Once cooked, allow the strawberries to cool for 30 minutes.

Meanwhile, whisk the cream to soft peaks. (Take care not to over-whip the cream, as it can separate.)

Divide the strawberries between four bowls, crumble over the shortbread fingers and dollop on a big spoonful of whipped cream.

SPICED APPLE CRUMBLE

SERVES 4-6

Who knew you could make crumble in a slow cooker?! I've taken my apple filling up a notch by lacing some gooey biscuit spread through the fruit layer, then the topping contains crumbled speculoos biscuits to echo those same warming, wintery spices. It's gorgeous on its own, but you could always add a glug of cream or a scoop of vanilla ice cream.

- Cooking time: 2 hours 30 minutes on high; or 5 hours on low
- Preparation time: 15 minutes
- Calories: 547 kcals per serving (based on 4 servings) or 412 kcals per serving (based on 6 servings)

For the apple filling

800g Bramley apples, peeled, cored and diced (about 4 medium apples)

1 tablespoon soft brown sugar

½ tablespoon cornflour

4 tablespoons smooth speculoos biscuit spread (I use Biscoff)

For the crumble topping

75g salted butter, at room temperature, plus an extra 5g to grease the pot

75g soft brown sugar

75g plain flour

75g speculoos biscuits, crumbled into some large and some smaller chunks

Rub a small amount of the butter all over the inside of the slow cooker pot.

In a mixing bowl, toss the apples with the sugar and cornflour until evenly coated.

Transfer the apples to the pot of the slow cooker, covering the base. Dot the biscuit spread over the apples.

To make the topping, combine the butter, sugar and flour in a bowl, rubbing it all together lightly with your fingers to form a sandy mixture. Fold the crumbled biscuits into the mixture. Scatter the topping over the layer of apples.

Cover the pot with the lid, positioning a clean tea towel between the pot and the lid to absorb some of the steam and stop the topping from becoming wet.

Set the slow cooker to 'cook' mode, then turn it either to high and cook for 2 hours 30 minutes or to low and cook for 5 hours.

COOK'S TIP

For another take on this crumble, mix salted caramel spread into the apples and crumble some crunchy, oaty biscuits (such as Hobnobs) into the topping.

CHERRY BAKEWELL COMPOTE

MAKES 1.4KG

Compote is a quick way of describing a jammy, fruit sauce. This compote pairs cherries with almonds – the flavours of a cherry bakewell tart. A compote is such an easy thing to have bubbling away in the slow cooker and, once made, it can be used in so many different ways. It's great mixed into Greek yoghurt with some granola or spooned over ice cream.

🔔 Cooking time: 5 hours on high; or 10 hours on low

⏲ Preparation time: 5 minutes (or longer if you're pitting fresh cherries)

♡ Calories: 174 kcals per 100g

1kg frozen dark sweet cherries (or 1kg fresh cherries, pitted)

400g jam sugar (with added pectin)

Juice of ½ lemon

1 tablespoon almond extract

3 tablespoons cornflour

Put all the ingredients (except the cornflour) in the pot of the slow cooker, then cover the pot with the lid.

Set the slow cooker to 'cook' mode, then turn it either to high and cook for 3 hours or to low and cook for 6 hours.

Remove 2 tablespoons of the cherry juices and combine with the cornflour in a small bowl to make a smooth paste. Stir the cornflour paste back into the cherry compote and cook, with the lid off, for a further 2 hours on high or 4 hours on low.

If not using straight away, leave the compote to cool and transfer to an airtight container. The compote will keep for up to 7 days when stored in the fridge.

COOK'S TIP

This cherry compote would even work well as the fruit layer of a crumble (see page 196) with some crushed amaretti biscuits folded into the topping.

STICKY TOFFEE PUDDING

SERVES 8–10

This steamed sponge pudding is a slow-cooker take on the classic sticky toffee. The pudding is fudgy and dense on its own, but it's even more amazing with the warm caramel sauce.

 Cooking time: 7 hours 30 minutes

Preparation time: 10 minutes

Calories: 472 kcals per serving (based on 10 servings)

For the pudding

200g Medjool dates, pitted

50g unsalted butter, plus extra for greasing

150ml boiling water

200g self-raising flour, sifted

200g dark brown sugar

1 teaspoon bicarbonate of soda

1 teaspoon ground cinnamon

1 tablespoon ground ginger

2 eggs, beaten

For the sauce

150g unsalted butter

150g soft light brown sugar

80ml double cream (I use Elmlea)

Pinch of sea salt flakes

COOK'S TIP

Cut any leftovers into slices and arrange them in a baking dish. Whip up an extra batch of caramel sauce and pour over the pudding. Reheat in the oven or air fryer to give the pudding a new lease of life.

Butter the inside of a 1.5 litre pudding basin and place a circle of parchment paper on the base.

Put the Medjool dates in a bowl with the butter and cover with the boiling water. Leave to soak for 15 minutes then blitz the dates in a high-speed blender (or using a handheld stick blender).

Combine the flour, sugar, bicarbonate of soda, ground cinnamon and ground ginger in a mixing bowl. Stir in the beaten eggs and the date purée. Mix to combine thoroughly.

Spoon the pudding batter into the greased basin. Cover the top of the bowl with a double layer of parchment paper and foil, making a pleat in the centre of the parchment so that the pudding has room to expand. Tie a length of kitchen string around the bowl, just under the rim.

Place the pudding basin in the pot of the slow cooker, then fill the pot with enough water to come halfway up the sides of the pudding bowl. Cover the pot with the lid.

Set the slow cooker to 'cook' mode, then turn it to high and cook for 7 hours.

Carefully remove the basin from the slow cooker, empty the water from the pot cooker and then dry it ready to make the sauce. Let the pudding sit while you make the sauce.

Add the butter, sugar, cream and a good pinch of sea salt flakes to the pot. Heat on low for 30 minutes, with the lid on, stirring every now and then, until the sauce is smooth and thickened.

Remove the foil and parchment paper from the pudding basin and carefully turn out the steamed pudding onto a flat plate. Portion out the pudding and serve with the hot caramel sauce poured over the top.

CHOCOLATE LAVA CAKE

SERVES 8

This self-saucing pudding is a bit of a magic trick. The boiling water sinks to the bottom of the pot, creating a rich chocolate sauce that sits underneath a light chocolate sponge! While this Chocolate Lava Cake is an all-in-one dessert, an extra drizzle of cream never hurts.

 Cooking time: 3 hours on high

 Preparation time: 10 minutes

Calories: 423 kcals per serving (without cream)

For the sponge

240g plain flour

1 tablespoon baking powder

200g sugar

40g cocoa

Pinch of sea salt flakes

230ml whole milk

60g unsalted butter, melted, plus a little extra for greasing

1 teaspoon vanilla extract

For the 'lava'

200g soft light brown sugar

50g cocoa

700ml boiling water

Lightly grease the inside of the slow cooker pot with a little butter.

To prepare the sponge batter, sift together the flour, baking powder, sugar, cocoa and sea salt flakes in a large mixing bowl. Make a well in the middle of the flour mixture and pour in the milk, melted butter and vanilla extract.

To prepare the 'lava', combine the sugar and cocoa in a bowl.

Spoon the sponge batter into the pot of the slow cooker, then sprinkle with the 'lava' mixture. Carefully pour over the boiling water. Cover the pot with the lid.

Set the slow cooker to 'cook' mode, then turn to high and cook for 3 hours.

COOK'S TIP

You can take the sponge up a notch by adding a handful of chocolate chips to the batter – white chocolate chips are always fun!

CRÈME CARAMEL

SERVES 6

A set vanilla custard, with a slight wobble, in a pool of caramel – yes please! There's a tiny bit of prep involved in making the caramel, but it's so worth it. This is a very elegant looking dessert, so it's one to pull out when you want to impress your guests.

 Cooking time: 2 hours 10 minutes plus 3 hours 30 minutes chilling

 Preparation time: 30 minutes

♡ Calories: 251 kcals per serving

For the caramel

120g sugar

For the custard

3 eggs, plus 2 egg yolks

100g sugar

500ml whole milk

1 teaspoon vanilla extract

COOK'S TIP

If don't have time to make the caramel from scratch, then just make the set vanilla custard and finish with some squeezy caramel drizzle sauce on top.

To prepare the caramel, put the sugar in a medium saucepan with 80ml water and warm it over a low-medium heat. Let everything bubble gently until the sugar has dissolved – do not stir the mixture, instead gently swirl it in the pan. Turn the heat up to medium and bring the mixture to a rapid simmer, then let it bubble for 8–10 minutes or until the caramel is amber in colour.

Carefully and quickly divide the caramel between six ramekins or dariole moulds. Let the caramel cool for 5 minutes while you make the vanilla custard.

In a large mixing bowl, whisk together the eggs, egg yolks and sugar. Next, whisk in the milk and vanilla, making sure everything is thoroughly combined.

Pour the custard mixture into the ramekins or darioles, on top of the caramel. Cover each dish tightly with foil (to stop them getting wet), then put them into the pot of the slow cooker. Pour enough boiling water into the pot to come half-way up the sides of the ramekins. Cover the pot with the lid.

Set the slow cooker to 'cook' mode, then turn to low and cook for 2 hours.

Let the crème caramel cool to room temperature for 30 minutes before chilling in the fridge for at least 3 hours.

To serve, use a knife to ease around the edge of the ramekin or dariole, invert the dish onto a plate and give it a few careful shakes to release the crème caramel.

CHOCOLATE ORANGE FUDGE

MAKES 64 PIECES

This is one of very few recipes in this book that you need to keep an eye, but it's only for an hour and the results are so worth it. As it's rich and dense, you only need a small piece or two of this fudge, which is great with a cup of coffee. It also makes a really lovely gift.

- Cooking time: 1 hour, plus 4 hours chilling
- Preparation time: 10 minutes
- Calories: 67 kcals per piece

120g soft brown sugar

200g dark chocolate, broken into pieces

300g milk chocolate, broken into pieces

1 x 397g tin condensed milk

Zest of 2 large oranges

Pinch of sea salt flakes

Put all the ingredients for the fudge (except the sea salt flakes) into the pot of the slow cooker and stir to combine. Cover the pot with the lid.

Set the slow cooker to 'cook' mode and turn it to low. Stirring every 15 minutes, cook the fudge mixture for 1 hour. If at any point the mixture starts to look grainy, beat it really hard with a wooden spoon.

Line a 20cm square baking tin with parchment paper.

Sprinkle a pinch of sea salt flakes into the fudge mixture, stir well, then scrape the mixture into the lined tin and level the surface.

Place the tin in the fridge and chill for 4 hours, or until set.

Once set, slice the block of fudge into 64 squares (8 x 8) using a very sharp knife.

COOK'S TIP

There are so many different ways you can flavour this chocolate fudge. How about adding some chilli flakes and ground cinnamon instead of using orange zest? Or what about scattering in a few chopped hazelnuts or even some mini marshmallows after you've poured the mixture into the tin to set? Or you could simply drizzle some melted white chocolate over the top of the fudge in the tin for a decorative effect.

MULLED CIDER

SERVES 8

This recipe is absolutely no-fuss – it's the perfect tipple to have ticking away in the slow cooker if you've got guests over during the holiday season. The brandy gives it a nice kick, but you can happily leave it out if you prefer something a bit tamer. Either way, it's great funnelled into a Thermos to enjoy at a firework display or during some Christmas carolling.

 Cooking time: 1 hour on low

 Preparation time: none

Calories: 176 kcals per serving

1.5 litres cider

500ml cloudy apple juice

100ml brandy (optional)

80g soft brown sugar

Zest of 1 orange

5 cloves

2 cinnamon sticks

Put all the ingredients for the mulled cider in the pot of the slow cooker, then stir to combine. Cover the pot with the lid.

Set the slow cooker to 'cook' mode, then turn it to low and cook for 1 hour, stirring every now and then to dissolve the sugar.

Switch the slow cooker to 'keep warm' mode or leave it on low to keep the cider mulling throughout the evening.

When ready to serve, ladle the mulled cider into heatproof glasses or mugs. Garnish each drink with a piece of the orange peel and a cinnamon stick, if you like.

BOOZY HOT CHOCOLATE

SERVES 6

I've called this Boozy Hot Chocolate because I love a small shot of Irish cream liqueur in my glass, but the hot chocolate itself is alcohol-free and entirely family friendly. For a gathering, you can make a big batch and keep it warm in the slow cooker, so it will tick over all by itself through an evening. By putting the liqueur straight into everyone's glass or mug, it can be adapted to individual taste. And feel free to go to town with the garnishes!

⏲ Cooking time: 1 hour 15 minutes on low

🍲 Preparation time: 5 minutes

♡ Calories: 373 kcals per serving (without cream or marshmallows)

4 tablespoons cocoa, plus extra to serve

4 tablespoons sugar

1 litre whole milk

100g dark chocolate, finely chopped

1½ tablespoons cornflour

150ml Irish cream liqueur (I use Baileys), plus extra to taste

To serve (optional)

Squirty cream

Mini marshmallows

Combine the cocoa and sugar in a jug. Add a splash of the milk and whisk to make a smooth paste. Slowly whisk in a little more of the milk, mixing until smooth.

Pour the cocoa mixture into the pot of the slow cooker. Add the remaining milk and the dark chocolate to the pot and whisk to combine. Cover the pot with the lid.

Set the slow cooker to 'cook' mode, then turn it to low and cook for 1 hour.

Remove 2 tablespoons of the hot chocolate from the slow cooker and mix with the cornflour in a small bowl and mix to a smooth paste. Whisk the cornflour paste back into the hot chocolate and cook, with the lid off, for a further 15 minutes.

For a boozy drink, put a 25ml shot of Irish cream liqueur in the bottom of each heatproof glass or mug. Fill the glasses or mugs with the hot chocolate and stir to blend. Test the hot chocolate and adjust to taste, adding a little more liqueur if you want a stronger drink.

Finish each drink with a swirl of squirty cream and a handful of mini marshmallows, if using, then a light dusting of cocoa.

apple juice: mulled cider 208

apples: pork stew with apples and cider 30

spiced apple crumble 196

aubergines: ratatouille 59

veggie moussaka 37

avocados: Mexican-style veggie chilli 42

bacon: cheesy ranch chicken 155

chunky baked beans 57

hunter's chicken 53

pork stew with apples and cider 30

smoky fish chowder 182

barbecue pulled pork buns 80

barbecue sauce 14

barbecue pulled pork buns 80

hunter's chicken 53

jerk-style chicken rice bowl 152

sloppy Joes 112

beans: chilli beef pasta bake 117

chunky baked beans 57

enchilada bake 123

harissa cod with chorizo and butter beans 133

jerk-style chicken rice bowl 152

Mexican-style veggie chilli 42

mushroom and mixed bean stew 38

beef: beef and mushrooms in peppercorn sauce 144

beef cannelloni 111

beef curry with potatoes and peanuts 79

beef stew with dumplings 24

beef topside 172

Bolognese sauce 108

cheeseburger pasta 115

chilli beef pasta bake 117

chunky beef chilli 76

crunchy beef chilli rice bake 130

enchilada bake 123

French onion and steak soup 46

keema curry 26

lazy lasagne 146

Madras-style beef curry 74

orzo ragù 165

pulled beef bagels 118

sloppy Joes 112

berries: stewed strawberries with shortbread and cream 195

biscuits: spiced apple crumble 196

stewed strawberries with shortbread and cream 195

Bolognese sauce 108

boozy hot chocolate 210

brandy: French onion and steak soup 46

mulled cider 208

bread: barbecue pulled pork buns 80

broccoli and cheddar soup 60

French onion and steak soup 46

sloppy Joes 112

broccoli: broccoli and cauliflower cheese 187

broccoli and cheddar soup 60

creamy salmon with potatoes 134

Thai green chicken curry 97

butter chicken 93

butternut squash: butternut squash and spinach daal 39

peri-peri mac n cheese with butternut squash 186

cabbage: barbecue pulled pork buns 80

Cajun-style chicken spaghetti 56

cake: chocolate lava cake 202

capers: creamy salmon with potatoes 134

caramel: crème caramel 204

    sticky toffee pudding 201

carrots: beef stew with dumplings 24

    beef topside 172

    chicken noodle soup 54

    fancy shepherds' pie 22

    lamb hot pot 19

    lazy lasagne 146

    leg of lamb cooked in red wine 179

    roast chicken 176

    sausage and onion casserole with mashed potatoes 27

    Thai green chicken curry 97

    veggie lasagne soup 62

    veggie sausage casserole with mashed potatoes 184

cauliflower: broccoli and cauliflower cheese 187

cheese 15

    beef cannelloni 111

    broccoli and cauliflower cheese 187

    broccoli and cheddar soup 60

    cheeseburger pasta 115

    cheesy ranch chicken 155

    chicken fajita pasta 139

    chicken fajitas 126

    chilli beef pasta bake 117

    chunky baked beans 57

    creamy paprika chicken with mushrooms 33

    creamy peri-peri chicken pasta 120

    creamy salmon with potatoes 134

    creamy sundried tomato and spinach gnocchi 164

    crunchy beef chilli rice bake 130

    Dauphinoise potatoes 188

    enchilada bake 123

    ham, mushroom and pea risotto 147

    hunter's chicken 53

    lazy lasagne 146

    marry me chicken 162

    orzo ragù 165

    pepperoni pizza orzo 50

    peri-peri mac n cheese with butternut squash 186

    pesto and pea pasta 138

    sausage ragù with rigatoni 28

    sloppy Joes 112

    smoky fish pie 34

    spinach and ricotta pasta shells 140

    tuna pasta bake 137

    Tuscan-style chicken orzo 128

    veggie lasagne soup 62

    veggie moussaka 37

    see also cream cheese; ricotta

cheeseburger pasta 115

cheesy ranch chicken 155

cherry bakewell compote 200

chicken: butter chicken 93

    Cajun-style chicken spaghetti 56

    cheesy ranch chicken 155

    chicken and chorizo jacket potatoes 156

    chicken fajita pasta 139

    chicken fajitas 126

    chicken noodle soup 54

    chicken rice bake with crispy onions 99

    chicken tikka rice bake 131

    Chinese curry chicken noodles 103

    creamy paprika chicken with mushrooms 33

    creamy peri-peri chicken pasta 120

    honey garlic chicken 94

    hunter's chicken 53

    jerk-style chicken rice bowl 152

    marry me chicken 162

    Moroccan-style chicken stew 161

    peri-peri pulled chicken 98

pollo picante 121

roast chicken 176

satay chicken curry noodles 91

sweet and sour chicken 100

Thai green chicken curry 97

Tuscan-style chicken orzo 128

chilli beef pasta bake 117

chilli prawn and prosecco linguine 168

chillies: beef curry with potatoes and peanuts 79

chicken noodle soup 54

chilli prawn and prosecco linguine 168

creamy tomato meatball pasta 116

jerk-style chicken rice bowl 152

lamb rogan josh 90

pollo picante 121

Thai green chicken curry 97

Chinese curry chicken noodles 103

Chinese-style pork spare ribs 85

chocolate: boozy hot chocolate 210

chocolate lava cake 202

chocolate orange fudge 207

chorizo: chicken and chorizo jacket potatoes 156

chorizo and prawn jambalaya 151

harissa cod with chorizo and butter beans 133

shrimp boil 167

chunky baked beans 57

chunky beef chilli 76

cider: mulled cider 208

pork stew with apples and cider 30

coconut milk: beef curry with potatoes and peanuts 79

butternut squash and spinach daal 39

jerk-style chicken rice bowl 152

pork and peanut noodles 82

satay chicken curry noodles 91

Thai green chicken curry 97

cod: harissa cod with chorizo and butter beans 133

smoky fish pie 34

cola: cola-glazed ham 175

compote: cherry bakewell compote 200

couscous: Moroccan-style chicken stew 161

ratatouille 59

stuffed peppers 70

cream cheese: broccoli and cauliflower cheese 187

broccoli and cheddar soup 60

Cajun-style chicken spaghetti 56

cheesy ranch chicken 155

creamy peri-peri chicken pasta 120

creamy salmon with potatoes 134

creamy sundried tomato and spinach gnocchi 164

creamy tomato meatball pasta 116

ham, mushroom and pea risotto 147

peri-peri mac n cheese with butternut squash 186

pesto and pea pasta 138

smoky fish pie 34

tuna pasta bake 137

Tuscan-style chicken orzo 128

creamy paprika chicken with mushrooms 33

creamy peri-peri chicken pasta 120

creamy salmon with potatoes 134

creamy sundried tomato and spinach gnocchi 164

creamy tomato meatball pasta 116

creamy tomato soup 68

crème caramel 204

crunchy beef chilli rice bake 130

curries: beef curry with potatoes and peanuts 79

butter chicken 93

keema curry 26

lamb rogan josh 90

Madras-style beef curry 74

Thai green chicken curry 97

custard: crème caramel 204

 D

dates: sticky toffee pudding 201

Dauphinoise potatoes 188

duck: shredded hoisin duck 177

dumplings: beef stew with dumplings 24

 E

eggs: crème caramel 204

    nut roast 183

    pork belly ramen 86

    shakshuka 67

    sticky toffee pudding 201

    veggie moussaka 37

enchilada bake 123

 F

fancy shepherds' pie 22

feta: stuffed peppers 70

fish: smoky fish chowder 182

    smoky fish pie 34

    see also cod; haddock; salmon

French onion and steak soup 46

fruit: cherry bakewell compote 200

    spiced apple crumble 196

    stewed strawberries with shortbread and cream 195

 G

gammon: cola-glazed ham 175

    pea and ham soup 49

garlic: garlic mushrooms with baby potatoes 69

    honey garlic chicken 94

gnocchi: creamy sundried tomato and spinach gnocchi 164

gochujang: pork and peanut noodles 82

Greek-style lamb shanks in white wine sauce 148

gruyère: Dauphinoise potatoes 188

 H

haddock: smoky fish pie 34

ham: cola-glazed ham 175

    ham, mushroom and pea risotto 147

    pea and ham soup 49

harissa paste: harissa cod with chorizo and butter beans 133

    stuffed peppers 70

honey: honey garlic chicken 94

    Moroccan-style chicken stew 161

hunter's chicken 53

 I

ingredients 14–15

Irish cream liqueur 210

 J

jacket potatoes: chicken and chorizo jacket potatoes 156

jam, raspberry: rice pudding 192

jerk-style chicken rice bowl 152

 K

keema curry 26

 L

lamb: fancy shepherds' pie 22

    Greek-style lamb shanks in white wine sauce 148

    lamb hot pot 19

    lamb rogan josh 90

    leg of lamb cooked in red wine 179

lazy lasagne 146

leeks: beef stew with dumplings 24

    ham, mushroom and pea risotto 147

pea and ham soup 49

sausage and onion casserole with mashed potatoes 27

veggie sausage casserole with mashed potatoes 184

lemon: Greek-style lamb shanks in white wine sauce 148

Moroccan-style chicken stew 161

roast chicken, 176

lentils: butternut squash and spinach daal 39

sweet potato and red lentil stew 40

Madras-style beef curry 74

marry me chicken 162

marshmallows: boozy hot chocolate 210

meatballs: creamy tomato meatball pasta 116

Mexican-style veggie chilli 42

miso: pork belly ramen 86

Moroccan-style chicken stew 161

mozzarella: beef cannelloni 111

cheeseburger pasta 115

crunchy beef chilli rice bake 130

enchilada bake 123

hunter's chicken 53

lazy lasagne 146

pepperoni pizza orzo 50

peri-peri mac n cheese with butternut squash 186

tuna pasta bake 137

veggie lasagne soup 62

mulled cider 208

mushrooms: beef and mushrooms in peppercorn sauce 144

creamy paprika chicken 33

creamy tomato meatball pasta 116

garlic mushrooms with baby potatoes 69

ham, mushroom and pea risotto 147

marry me chicken 162

mushroom and mixed bean stew 38

orzo ragù 165

pork belly ramen 86

noodles 14

chicken noodle soup 54

Chinese curry chicken noodles 103

pork and peanut noodles 82

pork belly ramen 86

satay chicken curry noodles 91

veggie chow mein 105

nuts: beef curry with potatoes and peanuts 79

Moroccan-style chicken stew 161

nut roast 183

pork and peanut noodles 82

see also peanut butter

onions: chicken rice bake with crispy onions 99

French onion soup and steak soup 46

orange: chocolate orange fudge 207

mulled cider 208

orzo ragù 165

pancakes: shredded hoisin duck 177

pasta 14

beef cannelloni 111

Cajun-style chicken spaghetti 56

cheeseburger pasta 115

chicken fajita pasta 139

chilli beef pasta bake 117

chilli prawn and prosecco linguine 168

creamy peri-peri chicken pasta 120

creamy tomato meatball pasta 116

lazy lasagne 146

marry me chicken 162

orzo ragù 165

pepperoni pizza orzo 50

peri-peri mac n cheese with butternut squash 186

pesto and pea pasta 138

pollo picante 121

sausage ragù with rigatoni 28

spinach and ricotta pasta shells 140

tuna pasta bake 137

Tuscan-style chicken orzo 128

veggie lasagne soup 62

pea and ham soup 49

peanut butter 14

beef curry with potatoes and peanuts 79

pork and peanut noodles 82

satay chicken curry noodles 91

peas: Chinese curry chicken noodles 103

ham, mushroom and pea risotto 147

keema curry 26

orzo ragù 165

pea and ham soup 49

peri-peri spiced rice 104

pesto and pea pasta 138

smoky fish pie 34

pepperoni pizza orzo 50

peppers: Cajun-style chicken spaghetti 56

chicken fajita pasta 139

chicken fajitas 126

chicken tikka rice bake 131

chilli beef pasta bake 117

Chinese curry chicken noodles 103

chunky beef chilli 76

chorizo and prawn jambalaya 151

creamy peri-peri chicken pasta 120

creamy tomato meatball pasta 116

crunchy beef chilli rice bake 130

enchilada bake 123

keema curry 26

lazy lasagne 146

Mexican-style veggie chilli 42

orzo ragù 165

pepperoni pizza orzo 50

peri-peri spiced rice 104

ratatouille 59

shakshuka 67

sloppy Joes 112

stuffed peppers 70

sweet and sour chicken 100

sweet potato and red lentil stew 40

veggie chow mein 105

veggie lasagne soup 62

veggie moussaka 37

peri-peri sauce 15

creamy peri-peri chicken pasta 120

peri-peri mac n cheese with butternut squash 186

peri-peri pulled chicken 98

peri-peri spiced rice 104

pesto and pea pasta 138

pineapple: sweet and sour chicken 100

pizza sauce: pepperoni pizza orzo 50

pollo picante 121

pork: barbecue pulled pork buns 80

Chinese-style pork spare ribs 85

pork and peanut noodles 82

pork belly ramen 86

pork stew with apples and cider 30

sausage and onion casserole with mashed potatoes 27

sausage ragù with rigatoni 28

potatoes: beef curry with potatoes and peanuts 79

beef stew with dumplings 24

chicken and chorizo jacket potatoes 156

creamy salmon with potatoes 134

Dauphinoise potatoes 188

fancy shepherds' pie 22

garlic mushrooms with baby potatoes 69

lamb hot pot 19

pea and ham soup 49

sausage and onion casserole with mashed potatoes 27

shrimp boil 167

smoky fish chowder 182

smoky fish pie 34

veggie moussaka 37

veggie sausage casserole with mashed potatoes 184

prawns: chilli prawn and prosecco linguine 168

chorizo and prawn jambalaya 151

shrimp boil 167

smoky fish pie 34

pudding: chocolate lava cake 202

rice pudding 192

sticky toffee pudding 201

pulled beef bagels 118

R

raisins: Moroccan-style chicken stew 161

ratatouille 59

rice 15

chicken rice bake with crispy onions 99

chicken tikka rice bake 131

chorizo and prawn jambalaya 151

crunchy beef chilli rice bake 130

ham, mushroom and pea risotto 147

jerk-style chicken rice bowl 152

keema curry 26

Mexican-style veggie chilli 42

peri-peri spiced rice 104

rice pudding 192

sweet and sour chicken 100

Thai green chicken curry 97

ricotta: spinach and ricotta pasta

shells 140

veggie lasagne soup 62

roast chicken 176

S

salmon: creamy salmon with potatoes 134

smoky fish chowder 182

smoky fish pie 34

satay chicken curry noodles 91

sausages: sausage and onion casserole with mashed potatoes 27

sausage ragù with rigatoni 28

veggie sausage casserole with mashed potatoes 184

shakshuka 67

shredded hoisin duck 177

shrimp boil 167

slaw: barbecue pulled pork buns 80

sloppy Joes 112

slow-cooker tips 10–13

smoky fish chowder 182

smoky fish pie 34

soup: broccoli and cheddar soup 60

chicken noodle soup 54

creamy tomato soup 68

French onion and steak soup 46

pea and ham soup 49

smoky fish chowder 182

veggie lasagne soup 62

speculoos biscuit: spiced apple crumble 196

spiced apple crumble 196

spinach: butternut squash and spinach daal 39

creamy sundried tomato and spinach gnocchi 164

pollo picante 121

spinach and ricotta pasta shells 140

Tuscan-style chicken orzo 128

stew: beef stew with dumplings 24

chunky beef chilli 76

Moroccan-style chicken stew 161

mushroom and mixed bean stew 38

pork stew with apples and cider 30

sweet potato and red lentil stew 40

stewed strawberries with shortbread and cream 195

sticky toffee pudding 201

stout: pulled beef bagels 118

stuffed peppers 70

stuffing: nut roast 183

sweet and sour chicken 100

sweet chilli sauce: chicken noodle soup 54

Chinese-style pork spare ribs 85

satay chicken curry noodles 91

sweet potatoes: sweet potato and red lentil stew 40

sweetcorn: chicken noodle soup 54

jerk-style chicken rice bowl 152

shrimp boil 167

smoky fish chowder 182

veggie chow mein 105

Thai green chicken curry 97

tomatoes, cherry: chilli prawn and prosecco linguine 168

creamy tomato soup 68

orzo ragù 165

pollo picante 121

stuffed peppers 70

tuna pasta bake 137

tomatoes, chopped: butternut squash and spinach daal 39

chicken and chorizo jacket potatoes 156

chorizo and prawn jambalaya 151

chunky baked beans 57

creamy tomato meatball pasta 116

crunchy beef chilli rice bake 130

lamb rogan josh 90

Madras-style beef curry 74

Mexican-style veggie chilli 42

orzo ragù 165

sausage ragù with rigatoni 28

shakshuka 67

sloppy Joes 112

sweet potato and red lentil stew 40

tomatoes, sundried: chicken and chorizo jacket potatoes 156

creamy sundried tomato and spinach gnocchi 164

Tuscan-style chicken orzo 128

tortilla chips: chunky beef chilli 76

crunchy beef chilli rice bake 130

tortilla wraps: chicken fajitas 126

enchilada bake 123

tuna: tuna pasta bake 137

Tuscan-style chicken orzo 128

vegetables: ratatouille 59

Thai green chicken curry 97

veggie chow mein 105

veggie lasagne soup 62

veggie moussaka 37

veggie sausage casserole with mashed potatoes 184

wine 15

beef topside 172

Bolognese sauce 108

fancy shepherds' pie 22

Greek-style lamb shanks in white wine sauce 148

ham, mushroom and pea risotto 147

lazy lasagne 146

leg of lamb cooked in red wine 179

marry me chicken 162

sausage ragù with rigatoni 28

ACKNOWLEDGEMENTS

As always, my first thank-you goes to Ru Merritt, Editorial Director at Ebury Press, for making every one of my books happen. Your support and advice throughout this process have been invaluable – I'm so grateful to have you in my corner. And the same goes for the entire Ebury team, including Francesca Thomson in publicity and Margarida Mendes Ribeiro in marketing for all their hard work in promoting my books.

Next, I need to thank Lisa Pendreigh for continuing to be the most patient and supportive editor. I simply could not have done all this without you. Thank you for helping me get all my recipes down on paper.

As the saying goes, we eat with our eyes. I have to thank the brilliant photography team who capture my recipes in photos you see on these pages. Thanks to my photographer Hannah Hughes, food stylist Katie Marshall and props stylist Lauren Miller, plus their assistants Sasha, Jess and Maisie – I've said this before but I couldn't love the photos any more.

To Studio Noel, thank you for the amazing design of the book. And to Lucy Gowans, thanks for bringing everything together on the pages.

And now to my family. I have to say the biggest thanks to my parents for always being there for me, supporting me and believing in me. I've learnt so much from you both! I'm so lucky to have a sister who is also my best friend – thank you for being my rock. And not forgetting my daughters. Everything I do is for you both, so I hope you're as proud of me as I am of you!

To James, thank you for listening to all of my thoughts and fears each and every day.

But the final – and hugest – thank you is to all of you, my followers and supporters. Thanks for following, liking, sharing and generally supporting me on my journey that has led to this, my third book. All of this has only been possible because of you.

ABOUT THE AUTHOR

Hayley Dean

With millions of views over recent years, the quick and easy slow-cooker and air-fryer recipes that Hayley shares online have really made their mark on anyone who is looking for easy, tasty meals to make at home. While Hayley may be best known for her air-fryer recipes, she actually used a slow cooker first and was an early adopter when it came to cooking with this handy appliance. Hayley continues to experiment with no-fuss, super delicious recipes made in the slow cooker that are enjoyed by all the family.

It was while she was working full time and raising her young family that Hayley first embraced the slow cooker. Entirely self-taught, Hayley has always been an experimental cook, often creating quick and easy versions of many of her favourite restaurant and takeaway dishes at home. She realised this kitchen gadget's potential to help serve up wholesome family food with the minimum of effort – for just a few minutes of your time doing a bit of prep, the slow cooker then does all the work and you're rewarded with a filling, tasty meal. She knows just how difficult it can be to eat well when you have little time to prepare meals, so Hayley's focus has always been on creating yummy recipes that are super easy to make.

Hayley's delicious, home-cooked, slow-cooker and air-fryer recipes have gained her an enthusiastic and loyal audience, with over 700k followers on Instagram and TikTok. Her slow-cooker recipes, such as Cheeseburger Pasta, Marry Me Chicken and Lasagne Soup regularly go viral and to date have received well over 10 million views. You can find Hayley and all the delicious food that she makes on Instagram at hayleys.world and on TikTok at hayleys.worldx.

Following on from Hayley's best-selling debut book, *How to Make Anything in an Air Fryer*, and her most recent cookbook, *How to Make Anything in an Air Fryer: Easy Dinners*, this latest collection of slow-cooker recipes includes a handful of Hayley's most-viewed, popular dishes along with a whole host of brand new ideas for no-fuss meals. You really can make anything in a slow cooker.

Ebury Press, an imprint of Ebury Publishing
20 Vauxhall Bridge Road, London SW1V 2SA

Ebury Press is part of the Penguin Random House group of companies whose addresses can be found at global.penguinrandomhouse.com

First published by Ebury Press in 2024

www.penguin.co.uk

A CIP catalogue record for this book is available from the British Library.

ISBN 9781529937992

Editorial Director: Ru Merritt
Project Editor: Lisa Pendreigh
Designers: Studio Noel and Lucy Gowans
Photographer: Hannah Hughes
Food Stylist: Katie Marshall
Props Stylist: Lauren Miller

Colour origination by Altaimage Ltd, London
Printed and bound in Germany by Mohn Media Mohndruck GmbH

The authorised representative in the EEA is Penguin Random House Ireland, Morrison Chambers, 32 Nassau Street, Dublin D02 YH68

Penguin Random House is committed to a sustainable future for our business, our readers and our planet. This book is made from Forest Stewardship Council® certified paper.